Conflict and Consensus in Higher Education

Conflict and Consensus
in Higher Education

Sinclair Goodlad

HODDER AND STOUGHTON
LONDON SYDNEY AUCKLAND TORONTO

Already published in the
Higher Education Today series
(general editor: W. Roy Niblett)

Universities between Two Worlds
  W. Roy Niblett

The Sciences, the Humanities and the Technological Threat
  Edited by W. Roy Niblett

The Open University from Within
  John Ferguson

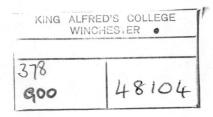
ISBN 0 340 18351 9

Printed in Great Britain for
Hodder and Stoughton Educational,
a division of Hodder and Stoughton Ltd, London,
by Hazell Watson & Viney Ltd, Aylesbury, Bucks

Contents

Preface

I have written this book at the invitation of Professor Roy Niblett. Its content owes much to the deliberations of two working parties, of which he was Chairman, which met regularly over a period of two years. A full record of all the meetings of these two working parties was kept by Mrs W. H. Hughes, Miss C. M. Eastwood, Miss E. Lamb, Mrs A. Penn-Bull, Miss T. M. Perfect, and Miss Susan Rawlings. This record, together with written discussion papers by working party members, supplied the raw material from which I was asked to write the book.

The names of those who participated in either or both of the working parties (and there was some overlap of membership) appear in a numbered list in an Appendix. The numbers throughout the text of the book indicate where particular thoughts or ideas are attributable to individual members speaking in the discussions or writing in the discussion papers. Where substantial sections of my text are paraphrased from discussion papers, specific mention is made in the text. By contrast, bibliographical references give author's name, date, and page number, and works cited are listed alphabetically by author in the bibliography.

The university is at the centre of the book's concern; but, in the two working parties there were also representatives of polytechnics, colleges of education, theological colleges, churches, business, industry, medicine and educational administration. In trying to report the discussions, I have strayed somewhat from the area of my immediate professional competence. It would have been relatively easy to examine the university in isolation and to do so from an explicitly sociological viewpoint, shielding myself where necessary with the appropriate jargon. But this would have been to negate the intention of a book such as this—which is to explore common ground between different disciplines and between universities and other institutions of higher education, and to do so in a style accessible to concerned people, of whatever profession or persuasion, who wish to understand the nature and purpose of higher education, particularly university education, in a plural society.

To Roy Niblett, I owe a lasting debt for having involved me in a deeply educative experience. My main debt, however, is to Frances Stevens, who was originally to have been co-author of the book. Chapter 2 is largely of her making, and other parts of the book owe much to the many hours of useful discussion I enjoyed with her and to her sensitive and discriminating comments on my text. I do, however, exonerate her and all those upon whose thoughts I draw for responsibility for what I have done with their material.

Finally it is my pleasure to thank Evelyn Lambert, who undertook the onerous task of typing and retyping the manuscript; Charles Knight, of Hodder and Stoughton, who was a very patient editor; and my wife, Inge, without whose constant support this book would never have been completed.

Sinclair Goodlad

CHAPTER ONE

Point of Departure

As a senior lecturer in Associated Studies (Literature and Sociology) attached to a department of Electrical Engineering in a college of Science and Technology (Imperial College, London University), I am a very impure academic specimen. The adulteration of my academic purity began during a lecture which I attended as an undergraduate student of English at Cambridge. A bibliographer of immense distinction spent an hour considering, for the edification of the English faculty, whether Shakespeare wrote (in *Hamlet*): 'O that this too too *solid* flesh should melt . . .' or rather 'O that this too too *sullied* flesh should melt . . .'. Yes, the actor must decide which variant to declaim. Yes, *Hamlet* is one of the richest creations in the English language. But . . . ? A few months after the Suez crisis, were there not matters of greater weight to be considered? And had I not defected to English from an A-level background in natural sciences in the hope of dealing with matters of human interest and concern?

My apprehension of the Absurd deepened during my first job as Lecturer in English Literature at St Stephen's College, Delhi University. Here were upper-middle-class Indians studying English primarily as a means to an end—the end being employment in the Indian Administrative Service or an international company such as Unilever. Within yards of encampments were refugees squatted in lean-tos made of beaten-out kerosene cans and cardboard boxes, one tried to teach Wordsworth to students who had never seen a daffodil, or *The Admirable Crichton* to Hindus who understood the caste system but were innocent of the mysteries of the English variant of it. Here was thought totally divorced from the possibilities of action. The more sensitive students felt the unworldliness of the situation. On the morning when the news broke of the death of Albert Camus in a car crash, small groups of students could be seen in the college in tears. *La Peste* was not on the syllabus: but Camus's Grand, heroically trying to write the perfect novel when not recording statistics of the plague, was a character who expressed in his life what many experienced.

Surrounded by a situation of unimaginable economic chaos, what was the value of studying literature? Undoubtedly there was value in literature itself: the response of Camus was itself indication enough of that. But was there any point driving intelligent young Indians through a syllabus similar to the English Tripos of Cambridge? Would it not be better for them to study the society in which they were living and whose problems they would eventually have to deal with? Should they not be acquiring techniques with which to work, rather than cultivating consciousness through the study of a foreign literature?

Needless to say, I was overreacting to the situation. Who could have predicted that a few years later herds of young Westerners would be migrating to India in search, apparently, of just the unworldliness which irritated me? No doubt they too would have rejected the Delhi degree syllabus; but because it was used instrumentally for access to the military–industrial–bureaucracy, not because it failed to confront what was most appalling in human terms—the poverty of the people.

Forced by a back injury to spend some time in hospital in the United Kingdom, I decided to enter the field of Liberal Studies in technical education. Here if anywhere there might be the opportunity of mixing thought (stimulated by literature) with action (made possible by technology). Accordingly, I went for a year as visiting lecturer to the Humanities Department at the Massachusetts Institute of Technology. But here the situation was equally bizarre. In the first week of term, bewildered freshmen were to be seen ploughing through Homer's *Odyssey*, the first Great Book in a one-year Introduction to Western Civilisation, a sort of Cook's tour of the high-spots of Western culture. As a colleague said: 'We feed them the sweetest nectar; but we just about blast their heads off with it.' The students' own phrase was even more evocative: 'Getting an education from MIT is like trying to drink from a fire-hose!' Once again, no effective link between thought and action. Not only did 'Western Civilisation' wash over students at a fantastic rate (four weeks were assigned to Ancient Rome!), but no connections were made with the mainstream technical studies. The situation at MIT has, of course, changed since 1962; but I came back to the United Kingdom still seeking a formula for linking what I considered best in humane studies with the obvious practical urgency of professional education.

At Imperial College, there was no Department of Humanities to offer the companionship of those who took it for granted that there was intrinsic worth in the study of literature. Indeed, I was the first non-scientist ever appointed to the faculty of Imperial College. Colleagues in the Electrical Engineering department were somewhat bewildered. For some, I had the virtues of a mascot—a conversation piece with which to entertain visitors (Oh, this is Goodlad, our culture merchant . . .); for others I was a sort of Mr Fixit to whom students with pronoun problems could be sent; for others I was a nuisance, if not a threat—a distraction from the serious business of circuit design. But, thanks to the patience and goodwill of three successive heads-of-department, Arnold Tustin, Willis Jackson, and John Brown, I was able to cooperate in a venture more nearly approaching what I dimly perceived to be the ideal: a scheme of group projects in which groups of four to six undergraduates, under the supervision of members of staff, studied some engineering problem in which considerations of men and money were as important as those of mathematics and materials. We even experimented with projects in which students visited developing countries to carry out work of direct practical utility while gathering information for their academic studies. Students helped with rural electrification work in Sierra Leone and in Zambia while studying the impact of electrification on rural economies. One group worked on a company contract in Venezuela while studying the development of a telecommunications network in a developing economy. Another group designed, and field-tested in Tunisia, a robust tape-playing device for use in fundamental education schemes in developing countries.

These projects were necessarily interdisciplinary and, by trespassing boldly (but I hope not irresponsibly) on other academic territory, I came to see the formidable obstacles of the departmental system which prevails in Western universities—and, as a marginal man, to see them perhaps more vividly than colleagues sailing briskly down the mainstream of a recognised discipline. My perception of the problem was also emerging in sociological terms because, while teaching at Imperial, I had been taking a Ph.D. in Sociology by part-time study at the London School of Economics.

A further twist to my thinking was given when I was telephoned by Alec Dickson, founder of Voluntary Service Overseas and honorary director of Community Service Volunteers. He had read about our overseas group projects and now confronted me with a question which with hindsight is blindingly obvious: why, if students can combine study with service overseas, can they not combine it with service in this country? We were marking time with the overseas group projects, not only because they were prodigiously expensive to run, but also because we were becoming concerned at the difficulties of adequately supervising projects at several thousand miles distance and worried lest we, through ignorance, were producing undesirable effects in the host countries. Our emphasis moved to action-oriented projects carried out in Britain. I have described the thinking behind them in *Education and Social Action* (1975), which also contains essays describing similar initiatives in other disciplines. The central question which these activities point to is that of combining the commitment of the individual student with the detachment which is implicit in the university approach to knowledge. Universities are thought-organisations, not will-organisations—as Moberly (1949, p. 39) put it.

It was at this time, when I was trying to work out the implications of what Alec Dickson was urging, that Roy Niblett invited me to join his working party on 'The Education of the Expert'. Here was a profoundly important activity, that of reflection, complementary to the more traditional university activities of research and of scholarship. Research requires the isolation of 'problems' defined within the frame of reference of identifiable disciplines; scholarship involves the refinement of observation within a limited area by means of precise techniques. Reflection, as undertaken by the working party and as continued in this book, is an attempt to consider certain complex problems in a wide perspective. It involves dangers of superficiality, of second-handness, of generality, even of factual error; but reflection is *primarily* concerned with clarifying assumptions and questioning what is often taken for granted. Unlike research, it deliberately and consciously ignores disciplinary frames of reference, the better to see how they aid or impede thought; unlike scholarship, it deliberately seeks connections between areas of study rather than sharpens focus on details within those areas. For these very reasons, it is a necessary complement to both research and scholarship.

Apart from the style of approach, the terms of reference of the working party were exactly in line with my preoccupations: 'to consider the ways in which the higher education of the expert given in universities and polytechnics should be modified so that, while no less efficient instrumentally as training, it may be more likely to produce among students both a developed sense of personal and social responsibility and a deeper and more comprehensive understanding of man's nature.'

Another working party was concentrating on a different but related issue: asking whether education in the humanities produces a general enlargement of sympathy and understanding, including sensitivity to moral, social, and aesthetic matters.

All the questions which I have found most difficult to deal with were being taken seriously—not pushed aside as so often happens. And when Roy Niblett asked me to write a book reporting some of the discussions and drawing a thread through them, I found myself with a task both exciting and daunting. How does one do justice to discussions—without plunging into the drabness of conference proceedings or the eccentricity of Thomas Love Peacock's novels? How does one re-present the thoughts of Seymour Betsky, Barbara Hardy,

Denys Harding and others wiser and more experienced than oneself without using their words? The chapters which follow are inevitably a compromise between mere reporting and writing a book of one's own. What I have done, I trust without causing too much offence to the working party members, is to pick out topics which reflect aspects of my own academic experience and use them to illustrate the theme which, although not always articulated, seemed to underlie much of the discussion—that of Authority.

One of the purposes of this book is, then, to explore the nature of authority in higher education with special reference to universities by examining certain aspects of higher education in which the central problem is to establish the most important of several very different goals for education and the criteria involved in determining the nature of the curriculum. It is not necessary to examine all aspects of university life and work to uncover the relevant issues for, just as a hologram contains in each of its parts the image held by the whole, so any one of the many activities of a university exhibits the basic dilemmas.

Conflict of various kinds is to be found in practically every aspect of higher education. Firstly, and most obviously, there is the conflict of goals for education. I have illustrated this with reference to professional education and to education in English literature. Then there is the conflict between different disciplines for comprehensive power: I have invented an 'interdisciplinary' discipline to illustrate the point that discpilines depend as much upon social groupings as upon correspondence to philosophic 'reality'. Thirdly, there is the conflict between 'objective' knowledge, with which all disciplines claim to deal, and 'subjectivity'. Fourthly, there is the potential conflict between personal commitment and institutional detachment as it appears in the curriculum and in the methods by which the curriculum is taught.

Some conflicts must be resolved and contained, if only for administrative reasons: this is the job of the educating institution. If the idea of a university, or any other educating institution, is to have continuity, the basis of its authority must be clearly understood and agreed to. But the steady drip of administrative exigencies can erode the shape of an institution beyond recognition just as surely as can compromise with fanaticism. In fact, for the university in a plural society, consensus may be more dangerous than conflict.

CHAPTER TWO

The Goals of Higher Education in a Plural Society

Four types of goal are commonly proposed for higher education. First, a socially defined goal of equipping individuals with the knowledge and skill suitable for given occupations—a manpower-planning goal manifest in the continuing debate about Government support for higher education and the balance to be achieved between different types of study. Committees on manpower planning promulgate social goals for education in the light of national need.

Second, there are the social goals of the 'consumers' of higher education—of students, and perhaps more importantly of their parents—for the social status which a degree validated by a university or the Council for National Academic Awards is believed to confer, and for a 'meal ticket'—a job qualification to be achieved as quickly and as efficiently as possible.

Third, there are the personal goals of some students to achieve independence in criticism or to acquire a philosophy of life.

Fourth, there are academic goals of unhurried and careful elaboration of theory supported by minutely detailed observation within the context of a discipline offering the support and respect of fellow scholars, and the possibility of 'international visibility'.

So that these goals may be defined with the precision that permits specific educational strategies, it is necessary to arrange them in some sort of order. In a plural society, this task is itself a problem. A plural society, in contrast to the Church-dominated society of mediaeval Europe, the Emperor-worshipping society of ancient Japan, or a modern Communist state, has no integrating and commonly accepted ethos but tolerates an immense variety of beliefs, life styles, moral standards, and forms of art. The goals of education in such a society will themselves be plural and may be incompatible with each other. The central problem in identifying the contribution to society of a university, or any other institution of higher education, is to distinguish important goals and to seek for the authority by which these goals may be placed in order of preference and realised in the curriculum. The search for order in this plurality of goals is beset with many problems arising from causes which include:

First, the accreditation of instrumental rather than absolute goals, or means rather than ends;

Second, the ease with which expertness can be validated as compared with other goals of education;

Third, the multiplication in contemporary society of so many different kinds of expertness;

Fourth, the defective humanising of the expert;

Fifth, the appropriation by the humanities of 'hard' disciplines; and

Sixth, the frequent aridity of humanistic studies.

A society with no universally accepted purposes or values finds it very much easier to recognise the products of education as a means to some other end, usually a fairly immediate one, and to evaluate them in terms of either personal experience or social role. The goals, therefore, are qualifications, instrumental in that they enable the student to attain a desired end which may or may not be of the same kind as the educational goal.

When academic goals are accredited chiefly as instruments—as qualifications—it is very difficult to decide on any order of preference in teaching aims or the content of the curriculum. Pushpin is as good as poetry. The difficulty is increased by the fact that it is much easier to validate expertness than the development of personal qualities. A student demonstrably is or is not a better analytical chemist than he was a year ago: but how to tell whether he is a better person?

If it is easier to accredit the expert—easier, that is, to set 'expert' than 'humane' goals—it may still be more difficult than it might seem, for there are so many different kinds of expert. If mere knowledge and skill are to be accredited, how is one to rank proficiency in soufflé-making, in solid state physics, in finance, or in 'social engineering'? By the complexity of the discipline, perhaps, by the personal qualities it requires and calls forth, by its use to society, or by its richness of association and suggestion? But this is to take us back into the realm of 'humane' qualities, and to blur the criterion of functional efficiency.

In many professions, the burden of required knowledge is so great, and the associated skills so difficult to acquire, that the student has (or feels he has) all he can do to survive the course. If students feel severe pressures within their specialism, humane values, if not entirely neglected, are likely to be the first casualty. The humanising of the expert constitutes a severe problem, not to be resolved by tinkering.

If it is worth resolving, this will have to be done by radical reconstruction of curricula and firmer definition of goals.

But there is also room for doubt about the humanity of 'humane' studies—that is, about their capacity to extend, discipline, and deepen reflection about the human condition. Where this doubt is justified, the deficiency observed is often attributable to two closely connected causes: first, the desire of those in arts faculties to avoid any suspicion of offering soft options, a desire which was particularly strong at a stage in higher education when scientific studies were rapidly increasing in number and difficulty, and for a time were proving alarmingly attractive—from the point of view of arts professors—to the ablest students; and second, the infection from the science side of new standards of objectivity, verifiability, scepticism, and supposedly value-free judgments. The first of these causes was accentuated by the emergence of new arts subjects.

The acceptance of a new study or group of studies as a valid university discipline is a complex process. One of the most important—or supposedly most important—criteria of academic respectability is 'rigour'. Another is coherent and at least partially exclusive content. English, the earliest of modern university studies, established in the nineteenth century under the dominance of the classics, speedily equipped itself with a rigorous (and quite inappropriate) 'classical' grammar, a body of 'classical' texts and an impressive *apparatus criticus*. All this was conducive to industry and scholarship, but only incidentally to sweetness and light and to the free play of thought around a subject.

Nearer our own time, the other cause—the infection of arts studies by 'scientific' methods and standards—has been the more considerable. As science grew in power and prestige, its methods became the aspiration not only of scientific but of all studies. At its extreme, this tendency resulted in the birth of new sciences, such as linguistics, from the arts themselves.

The difficulty of finding purposes with any degree of comprehensiveness for higher education in the modern world is to be expected in a plural society, which can very well assess the efficiency of specific and limited means to specific and limited ends, but is unable to place the ends themselves in a context of agreed values. In such a situation, there is a tendency to rate effectiveness very highly, raising it almost to the status of an end in itself. Competence with 'means' becomes an end.

At first sight, then, it seems much easier to set goals for the training of the expert than for education in the humanities. But confidence vanishes when any but the most temporary and immediate goals are sought. Disturbing questions of right and wrong, folly and wisdom, beauty and ugliness, waste and preservation, occur and recur. Does an architect take any commission he can get, regardless of its aesthetic standards, or its effects on the environment? Has a South African physiologist any special duty to give the lie publicly to the theory, often used to urge the impossibility of educating Africans and whites together, that African girls reach puberty significantly earlier than white girls? Nurses are known to have refused to work, or even to have left the profession, when required to assist at abortions in which the embryo is on the verge of being a viable foetus. There is now a 'conscience clause'. But what element in a nurse's training equips her with the means to make a decision? Against this line of thought may be argued, first, that, carried logically forward, the same principles as actuate the architect should actuate, no more and no less, the brick-layer who is employed by the builder who is employed by the archi-tect, or that the worker in the factory has some responsibility for the machine for which he makes components, as real if not as extensive or manifest as that of the designer of the machine. Second, it may be said that the decisions taken by the architect, the physiologist, and the nurses are taken by them as men and women, not as professional people. Certainly it is necessary to have standards of aesthetic quality, or veracity, or respect for life. But people acquire these first as personal standards, and then apply them to the work they are doing.

These are not easy matters. Such arguments, if maintained, might lead to the conclusion that the developing of awareness and judgment has no necessary place among the aims of higher education. If such development is desirable, it is to be desired as much for ordinary men and women as for the few who have the advantage of higher educa-tion. It is, moreover, through the religious and other attitude-forming institutions of society, claiming concern with all rather than with a specialised group, that values are and should be acquired. In consider-ing the first argument, it may be agreed that awareness and judg-ment are desirable for all. But it must also be said that, through the very elaboration and the demanding nature of his training, the expert has opened up to him a far greater range of possibilities (and, there-fore, of necessity, for decision-making) than is available to those who use his knowledge or carry out his instructions. He also holds the initial power—the power of design and execution: he therefore needs commensurate training in evaluation and responsibility. The answer to the second argument is on similar lines, but may be put more posi-tively. For, it may be said, the training of the expert is so rich in its complexities, so charged with potentialities of human significance, that to fail to exploit these qualities is to miss an important educa-tional opportunity, and to leave in naivety and ignorance a person who may have considerable influence in human affairs.

(a) *The nature of the university's teaching responsibility in a plural society*

Can a plural society be said to have a common culture? And if it has, what aspects of that culture should be preserved in education?

A notable feature of a plural society is the frequent feeling of revolt and despair induced by rapid social or technological change—for there is, by definition, no commonly accepted way of evaluating such changes. Questions of social justice, questions of social function, and ultimate questions, sometimes of a metaphysical nature, concerning the meaning and significance of life are, perhaps, nearer the surface of life in a plural society than in any other type of society. Certainly, in higher education, such questions may be initiated by either the teachers or the taught. They may, and perhaps should, become an essential part of what Ben Morris has called 'education as transaction'. But they may also, and rightly, constitute a good deal of the internal debate of each group. Thus they may provide goals for higher education in the sense that, where they are compelling preoccupations of students, the answering of them gives direction and significance to these students' academic tasks. They can also, when asked in the internal debate of teachers, lead to the better definition of teaching purposes.

The fundamental questions which may exercise students can be raised and discussed in many contexts. For example, the ethics of medicine are generally learned from the codes of the peer group and by tradition rather than through direct instruction. If, however, in the course of the medical student's formal education, the ethical implications of drug prescription, of kidney machines, of particular psychiatric techniques, are examined by senior and junior members together, then fundamental questions are entering into the educational transaction.

But should the teacher deliberately raise questions like these which blur the boundaries between the special social roles for which professional education is a preparation? The role of the teacher has traditionally been that of mediator and conserver, and his task to initiate the young into the culture. His role is different in our time, partly because of the pluralism of society, partly because the growth of new knowledge and techniques makes it necessary for the pupil rather to be prepared for the unknown than to be introduced to the wisdom of the past. A noticeable feature of our culture is the insecurity of teachers at all levels of education and the uncertain nature of their authority. No longer supported by what might be called a professional sodality, they may be tempted into a dangerous reliance on 'charisma'. Yet the present conditions provide both the opportunity and the necessity to establish a new kind of authority and point to new goals.

It is all too easy for the teacher, whether in school or in university, to live professionally according to the conventions and attitudes of a past generation. But the authority of teachers in both planning and practice is called in question when what may be taken for granted is no longer clear. What is the authority of the teacher in the culture of a plural society? It is perhaps to be sought in mutual respect between teachers and taught—a glad and willing alliance of free people.

It is becoming increasingly necessary for the teacher (who can no longer rely on tradition or *force majeure*) to understand the social structure within which education, particularly technological education, takes place. Moreover, if we do not know what the specialisms of the future will be, or are uncertain of the nature of the expert's role, we must be honest and train in a way that makes clear that we are not quite sure what we are training people for.(8) Easy to say—hard in its implications. Courage and self-discipline are involved in such positive tolerance of uncertainty. Such tolerance of uncertainty —a positive tolerance which does not mean the absence of beliefs— is the positive thrust of pluralism.

Not only the relationship of the individual teacher to his culture— the relationship of the higher education system itself to the total culture must be examined. It is worth recalling that the word 'authority' has the same root as the word 'author'—one who brings anything into being. A university has traditionally been seen as agency for the discovery of knowledge as well as for its transmission. Is it, more importantly, what Charles Davies was quoted (by John Coulson) as saying—'The creative centre of our culture'?(5)

John Coulson suggested that if we can justify the place of theology in the university, we shall succeed in showing what its function is in the culture of a plural society. And so, one might think, with all the other university disciplines—which implies, surely, teaching them so as to place them consciously within their cultural setting.

This is the crux: in a plural society, on whose authority is the cultural setting defined?

To take one example: the education of the technical expert may be seen to be primarily a social and political, rather than an educational, question. For this very reason, educationalists need to recognise clearly the social and political framework within which they are working if they are to be in a position to recognise which are the desirable directions of advance.(8)

The relationship between higher education and society as a whole is, in fact, unstable and paradoxical. Higher education is no longer the prerogative of a social, and is decreasingly that of an intellectual, elite. It is simultaneously demanded and resented. And no one is sure whether its function is primarily adaptive, or innovative and creative.

(b) *Must higher education in a plural society be ideologically neutral?*
Without an ideological framework, it is very difficult to find criteria
by which to evaluate cultural or educational goals. At the same time,
higher education itself, particularly university education, is the emin-
ently appropriate realm for scrutinising ideas, philosophies, and value
systems, and for generating new ones. Whose interests does it exist to
serve? And how are those interests defined?

A model of a positive relationship between education and society is
to be found in Soviet culture and education. Suggesting that it is impossible to evaluate an educational system apart from the society it
reflects and serves, John Grayson listed the following characteristics
of contemporary Russian education:

Its purposes are social, not individual;
It is secular;
Its bias is scientific and utilitarian;
It has a universal-human foundation;
It emphasises the theme of Russian nationality;
Productive work is seen as part of general education.(12)

Clearly, it will not do simply to compile a contrary list and take it
as a model of education in a plural society. The matter is a good deal
more complex than that. A plural society is certainly not ideologically
neutral. If a 'containing' ideology is required, a unifying social myth
(concerning what may be taken for granted), could pluralism be
plural society's own super-myth?(6)

Perhaps the nearest approach to an answer is to be found not in our
own day at all, but in Keats's well-known words about negative capability: 'I mean *Negative Capability*, that is, when a man is capable of
being in uncertainties, mysteries, doubts, without any irritable searching after fact and reason' (Keats, 1935, p. 72). This is not so very far
from the words of an author in other respects worlds removed—
those of Bernard Shaw in his preface to *St Joan*:

'I have before me the letter of a Catholic priest. "In your play" he
writes, "I see the dramatic presentation of the conflict of the Royal,
Sacerdotal and Prophetical powers, in which Joan was crushed. To
me it is not the victory of any one of them over the others that will
bring peace and the reign of the saints in the Kingdom of God, but
their fruitful interaction in a costly but noble state of tension." The
Pope himself could not have put it better; nor can I. We must
accept the tension and maintain it nobly without letting ourselves
be tempted to relieve it by burning the thread.' (Shaw, 1965, p. 623)

Is this the ideological goal of higher education in a plural society?

Many people, of course, constantly wish to relieve tension, if necessary by burning the thread. They will perceive in contemporary

society not a striving for the goals of negative capability or fruitful interaction, but rather a prevalent sense of goallessness. Sometimes this sense is attended by no uneasiness but by a kind of comfortable irresponsibility. At other times it is productive of anxiety, which generates a great desire to find goals and make them explicit. Even scientific or technical goals cannot be treated as self-evident: they have to be decided upon from among the choice of options in the light of specifiable criteria.

Though it may be that a concern for more distant goals is manifesting itself today, a common reaction to goallessness is to look for immediate and concrete objectives. To many people, one of the most manifest goals of education is to get a good job. If higher education is undertaken with this goal and this goal alone in mind, there can be great discouragement and frustration when the highly trained person cannot get the specialist work for which he has prepared himself. Manpower and consumer demands are frequently out of step with each other. And when specialisms, in terms of employment, are poorly defined, it is more difficult than ever for young people to decide between a specialist and a broad education. They face the hazard either of being unable to get the work for which they have been trained, or finding their training largely irrelevant to the 'real' problems of their job.

(c) *The interplay of public and private goals*

Nearer goals are determined by more distant ones, which may be divided into those concerned with the purposes (not always consciously perceived) of society, and those concerned with the personal development of the individual. It is hardly necessary to point out that the two parts are complementary. Society has a plurality of sometimes incompatible goals, or very immediate goals, or no goals at all. Higher education is part of society, so its teachers and students are likely to show the same characteristics. Yet it is also the function of higher education in some respects to stand aside from the society of which it is part. Perhaps it has become the duty of teachers in higher education to teach *about* goals, to incorporate deliberately a teleological element in their studies. How is this to be done? One part of the task is to maintain a high level of educational discussion. Dialectic is an ancient and honourable approach to wisdom, and never more necessary than now. The debate must be maintained—but it is difficult, both because of the largeness of the field, and because of the fissiparous nature of society. It is tempting to seek relief either in imprecision or in a concern with the more limited and accessible aspects of education. Much valuable and informed discussion among educationists and others is related much more to short-term, essentially domestic, issues than to the longer-term consequences of our present situation. When decisive changes in education are being proposed and executed, the major questions to which they should be related are often lost amid concern with organisation, economics and control.(8)

But within the whole higher education debate is hidden a fundamental conflict between educational attitudes: between a sophisticated and clever opportunism and the strenuous and disciplined maintenance of stable and critical principles of evalution. It is obvious why value-questions are avoided: they are disturbing, and they provoke conflict. Who are the important people who help to establish values? How is the student to get away from the domination of the teacher? Do we educate for social roles or for the 'whole' person? Are we projecting a myth of the polymath as the perfect man? Does our education of experts alert them to self-critical reflection? How may the young man know whether he wishes to be an expert? What relationships can be established between academic study and personal and social experience? How can we create conditions conducive to questioning the values and image of a life worth living? These are exceptionally difficult questions and easily neglected in discussions of higher education.

In the face of manpower-planning goals, and 'consumer' goals which see higher education mainly in instrumental terms, goals concerned with personal development can soon be lost to sight. Perhaps the key to further development of the idea of the personal in a plural society lies in the nature of the types of encounter encouraged by higher education. Some educational encounters increase a student's dependence on his teachers and upon their modes of thought; others encourage independence. One aspect of today's pattern of revolt, whether in higher education or in industry, is a blind assertion of the personal; a protest against the anonymity and facelessness of 'the others' and the threatened annihilation of the self. Objectivity as an educational goal has its stern virtues, and also its hazards. Subjectivity too must have its due status.

Sterilisation or killing is implicit in the analytical process: strictly, and necessarily, 'we murder to dissect'. Amid the compensatory rush to magic, to fundamentalism, perhaps to totalitarianism, educators need to rediscover the imagination. It is not for nothing that Blake speaks straight to contemporary youth. The imagination is closely allied to what James Robertson called prophecy, the task of which is, he said, to illuminate contemporary history, to clarify crucial options, and to summon man to the responsible stewardship of his world.(29) Imagination and prophecy are the true centre of general education, which should come readily from within specialist studies.

A plural society, then, cannot place goals or ends for higher education in order within a context of agreed values, for in a plural society it is not certain on whose authority the cultural setting is defined. For this very reason, universities can be seen to offer their own ideological goal—that of accepting and maintaining the tension between competing goals without burning the thread. To be effective in maintaining this tension, universities, and in their own special ways other institutions of higher education, must recognise the types of authority appealed to by proponents of the competing goals. In evaluating these forms of authority, universities must fall back upon a standard of judgment of their own—in fact, *themselves* appeal to a form of authority. The laying bare of crucial options in a context critical and yet permissive, and pointing to uncertainties implicit in a field of learning, is, I shall argue, the central task of higher education.

These are high-sounding words; their meaning is best perceived through detailed attention to specific problems. Such problems may be examined in the educating of professional chemists and of students of English Literature.

There is a widespread suspicion that the education of intending professionals is more in the nature of training than of exposure of the individual to crucial options. The commissar must be trained in the bureaucratic and technical techniques of society to operate efficiently. By contrast, the yogi, in the present context the student of the humanities, is believed to enjoy a 'liberal' education which gives him freedom of thought. In the first case, authority is external; in the second, it is internal. In practice, however, matters are not nearly so simple. Authority is a complex concept.

CHAPTER THREE

The Freedom of the Trained

There is a potential conflict in the education of intending professionals between training for a prescribed role, validated by the practising profession, and the wide-ranging, institutionalised scepticism and detachment which is implicit in the traditional university approach to knowledge. To operate effectively as 'experts', professional people need to have consensus about what constitutes knowledge and clear professional guidelines to distinguish moral questions from technical ones. But both the theoretical preoccupations of disciplines as conceived of in universities, and the day-to-day requirements of professional practice, continually threaten to blur the edges of professional autonomy. Experts may wish to be on top; society may wish to have them on tap. Both views about the role of experts in society have led to proposals that the education of the expert should include education about social values. Such education, however, is likely to create more conflicts than it resolves and to provoke questions concerning the authority of professional or expert knowledge. This chapter, therefore, examines the criticisms which are often made of technical education and the remedies which are proposed, and seeks to expose the implicit issues concerning authority.

Popular ideas about the expert have oscillated between a positive image and a negative one. Irrational confidence in the supposed incorruptible excellence of experts is counterbalanced by an equally irrational mistrust or fear of experts. Popular fiction is littered with mad geniuses—Faustus, Dr Strangelove, Dr No—whose monomania threatens all mankind if their twisted impulses are not kept in check by men representing ordinary mortals. Expertise is usually shown to be unhealthy; even the gentle professor who saves society from destruction by monsters or maniacs, requires the suitor of his lovely daughter as a foil of human scale.

Who are the experts and what are they for? The concern of this chapter is not with the twisted genius of science fiction who seeks to mould society cynically for his own delight, but rather with the expert most readily recognised as a member of a learned profession. Schein (1972, chapter 1) and Elliott (1972, p. 96 *et seq*) have conveniently listed the ideal-typical characteristics of a profession: based on a specialised body of knowledge; requiring a prolonged education; making judgments on the basis of general principles; characteristically doing so in non-routine situations; providing a service for clients; making no moral judgments of clients; forming a recognisable occupational group because work and occupation are a central life interest; recognising only members of the professional occupational group as entitled to judge a member's actions; itself as a body defining the criteria of membership.

Some occupations obviously satisfy this picture more fully than others and there can be no sharp boundary between professions and other occupations. But the possession of and institutional celebration of expertise is of fundamental importance. It is on this characteristic of a profession that certain contemporary criticism concentrates. A typical comment is that contained in the *Making of a Counter Culture* (1971, pp. 6–8) by Theodore Roszak.

'In the technocracy, nothing is any longer small or simple or readily apparent to the non-technical man. Instead, the scale and intricacy of all human activities—political, economic, cultural—transcends the competence of the amateurish citizen and inexorably demands the attention of specially trained experts. Further, around this central core of experts who deal with large-scale public necessities, there grows up a circle of subsidiary experts who, battening on the general social prestige of technical skill in the technocracy, assume authoritative influence over even the most seemingly personal aspects of life; sexual behaviour, child-rearing, mental health, recreation, etc. In the technocracy everything aspires to become purely technical, the subject of professional attention. The technocracy is therefore a regime of experts—or of those who can employ the experts.

. . . the technocracy is that society in which those who govern justify themselves by appeal to technical experts who, in turn, justify themselves by appeal to scientific forms of knowledge. And beyond the authority of science, there is no appeal.

Understood in these terms, as the mature product of technological progress and the scientific ethos, the technocracy easily eludes all traditional political categories. Indeed, it is characteristic of the technocracy to render itself ideologically invisible.'

Criticism concentrates not only on the fact that such proliferation of professionalised expertise represents a form of alienation, but also on the fact that schools and colleges increase the tendency of the job-market to make skills scarce and to turn knowledge into a form of personal possession (see, for example, Ivan D. Illich, 1971.) Is it any part of the business of universities to challenge, mitigate, or reverse this tendency? As major contributors to professional education, should universities simply impart technical knowledge; or should they, rather, systematically expose students to value-questions which locate technical knowledge socially? This chapter examines the typical characteristics of a course of professional education, the criticisms which have been made of it, and the remedies which have been pro-posed. The suggested remedies raise difficult questions concerning the authority by which the role of the professional is defined.

(a) *Strengths and weaknesses of professional education in Chemistry*

Dr P. J. T. Tait offered 'some reflections on the education of the scientific expert'(35) which dealt with a typical chemistry course. His paper provides a suitable model of professional education because chemistry not only involves the same type of intellectual fascination as do other physical sciences, but also, through the way it is taught to undergraduates in universities, invites the type of criticism which may be generalised to other fields of professional education. First, there-fore, the promise; then, the problems.

Tait argued that the fascination of chemistry arises from a subtle interaction of a number of well-known facets of the principles of science and certain basic modes of operation of the human mind. There is, he argued, an obvious connection between a capacity for curiosity and basic human intelligence; without innate curiosity there can be no true scientific enquiry.

Secondly, he distinguished the capacity to look for and identify relationships. Curiosity is obviously not enough in itself: it provides a driving force. It is the ability to see the connections which matters; the capacity to see similar things in different phenomena. This search for connections is a fundamental part of the fascination of chemistry. Thirdly, there is the capacity for analysis. Analysis is very much the working tool of the scientist. It gives substance to curiosity and to the search for connections; it is in effect a mode of operation. The chemis-try student is concerned with such questions as: what are the im-portant variables? Which are dependent? Which are independent? The whole is seen in terms of the constituent parts and, Tait com-mented, it is of interest to reflect that the approach of the arts graduate is often the opposite of this.

Fourthly, there is the fascination of change. It is a fundamental quality of the human mind, even in early childhood, to feel great interest in change of position or in rearrangement. Chemistry is con-cerned with both, and chemical terminology is rich with such terms as velocity, equilibrium, kinetics, etc. Moreover, most common and elementary reactions can be used as examples of these concepts and students meet them early in their chemical careers.

Finally, chemistry involves the opportunity to make and create. The preparation, isolation, and analysis of a product bring their own peculiar satisfaction in the scientific enterprise. The opportunity to make some rare compound (unknown to nature) may be offered to undergraduates at an early stage in the chemical laboratory. Science, and chemistry in particular, has a strong appeal because many of its elemental modes of thought are in harmony with the basic human quest to discover identity.

With such promise, what then are the characteristic criticisms of university science courses?

Firstly, scientific courses are frequently criticised for being too cramped and narrow in outlook. Scientists are accused of being unaware of their cultural and aesthetic heritage and university science courses are accused of failing to provide the necessary encounters. Scientists, it is said, receive a training, but little of an educational experience.

Secondly, it is asserted that any change in curriculum has been achieved by the progressive addition of yet more new material to an already over-congested syllabus. There are increasing instances of so-called subsidiary subjects being reorganised so as to become mere extensions of the main courses. The ideal of exposing students to fresh and new modes of thinking is being either abandoned or put into cocoon for some future and more convenient period.

Thirdly, industrialists have joined the chorus of criticism. Present science courses are considered to contain little of industrial relevance, and the assertion is even made that a Ph.D. training positively harms the graduate's industrial potential. Rigid modes of academic thought and aspiration are seen as leading to inflexibility and even immobility when the graduate is finally confronted with a 'real' problem.

Fourthly, there has arisen a feeling that much of science and technology is irrelevant as far as many of the pressing problems of life are concerned. Since the war, science has been oversold, and has failed to 'deliver the goods'. We are still confronted with poverty, all kinds of social ills, and the threat of global war. Physical pollution becomes a semi-religious concept—almost like sin. Many critics maintain that present scientific education courses provide no real opportunity for even an acquaintance with these problems.

In recent years, the over-production of many kinds of scientists has meant that many graduates have been compelled to look outside their primary field of study. The fifth type of criticism is that whilst many science undergraduate courses provide excellent raw material—the hewers of wood and the drawers of water—for the professor's research school, they provide but a poor foundation and a scanty preparation for a 'self-fulfilling role' in some other field.

Tait outlined certain operational characteristics of a typical chemistry course which give rise to the criticisms.

Firstly, the high lecture and supervision load. There may be very few 'free' periods in a working week when a student can follow his thinking where it leads him. Secondly, much time is spent in the laboratory. Clearly, an experimental subject demands much laboratory time, but many critics feel that the expenditure of time is excessive. Thirdly, science courses frequently have a high 'fact' content. Chemistry, for example, is an enormous subject, and it is still fashionable to attempt to cover all 'important and essential parts'. Fourthly, singleness-of-mind is a key quality for success and mental energy and stamina are needed to survive in such a course. Little time and energy can be left over from such an intensive course for other forms of cultivation of the mind. Fifthly, a typical science course is convergent in nature and has a vocational bias. These characteristics of themselves may not be vices; but if they inhibit other forms of activity they may be.

It is worth pausing to review some of these comments and criticisms in the light of the different types of goal for higher education examined in the second chapter—national 'manpower' goals, 'consumer' goals, personal goals, and academic goals.

(b) *The failure of specialist education to meet the major goals of higher education*

Firstly, several government reports have pointed to the mismatch between the production of scientific experts and national need (Swann, Dainton, McCarthy). All have urged broadening of the education of scientists and engineers to include exposure to social, political, economic, and such like questions of human values. It is not only the rapid obsolescence of technical knowledge which causes anxiety; increasingly, as Schein (1972) and others have pointed out, professional posts are held in group practices and scientific and technological experts are very likely to work in teams. There are many complex and obstinate social problems—urban ghettoes, environmental pollution, mass transport—which require the activity of professionals who appreciate one another's forms of expertise and who can collaborate effectively. The precision of scientific and technological activity often involves its practitioners in concern with only a minute part of a system which is being developed. While the so-called 'systems approach' advocated by such people as Ramo (1969) may commend itself, it is commonly argued that the education of professionals—particularly those whose profession will involve scientific or technological expertise—should incorporate material drawn from subjects outside the main disciplines of science and technology.

Secondly, 'consumers' of technical education are clearly dissatisfied with the product. This dissatisfaction is reflected in the fall in the number of applications for courses in certain highly specialised disciplines such as metallurgy. The reasons for the periodic decline in popularity of one discipline or another are hard to find, and it may, therefore, be profitable to consider the failure of certain courses to meet 'consumer' goals simultaneously with the closely-related possibility that they may fail to meet personal goals. Even at such a bastion of specialist education as Imperial College, there has been increasing 'consumer' interest in the provision of non-technical studies as part of the science or engineering degree course. R. Mohan *et al.* (1970) report a survey of student opinion and give figures indicating interest in different types of study. The fact that 96 per cent of a thousand undergraduates who completed a questionnaire wanted non-technical courses to be made available is of sufficient interest in itself; but perhaps more interesting are some of the verbatim comments of science and engineering undergraduates which the article quotes:

'*Geologist*: It's about time we learnt to use our scientific knowledge in relation to society and domestic affairs.

Physicist: . . . education is the stuff of which civilisation is made and no science course can be anything like a complete education. It is, of course, a good mental training and any civilised society must possess a large number of highly trained technologists and scientists. I demand more than science!

Civil Engineer: The idea of having compulsory non-technical subjects in our courses is a very good and essential one. The narrowmindedness of the average student at Imperial College is quite appalling. One hopes that the theory of going to university to be educated rather than be fed data like a computer is not entirely erroneous, and these courses would certainly help to improve the position.

Civil Engineer: The need for a more balanced education of science students is both pressing and obvious.'

There were of course students who bucked this trend and the article quotes the views of one such:

'*Physicist*: I came to Imperial College for the simple reason that there were no auxiliary courses of humanities, and social sciences, etc. Had I wanted them I would have gone elsewhere! The fact is that I am a narrow-minded scientist and wish to remain so.'

Evidence of the dislike of specialisation was also discovered by the Schools Council sixth-form survey *Sixth Form Pupils and Teachers* (1970). Asked whether 'If the need to get higher marks in exams had been less acute it would have been desirable to spend more time on general studies', 43 per cent of sixth-formers (but 70 per cent of 3000 ex-sixth-formers) said yes. Again, the ex-sixth-formers were asked 'Whether they would have preferred a more specialised course or a wider course covering more subjects or whether they thought their course was about right.' Forty-three per cent would have preferred a wider course, 9 per cent a narrower, 48 per cent were happy; the same figure of 43 per cent went for those of the ex-sixth-formers who had gone on to university.

Does professional education fail to meet academic goals? University education has generally been held to be unlike school education or narrowly vocational education because it is concerned with the use and management of explanatory languages (or modes of thought) and not descriptive languages. Vocational education, by contrast, is designed to fit a man to fill a specific place in a current manner of living or to satisfy a current demand. This in itself need not make a subject unsuitable for study in the university—even if the calculations of manpower planners go seriously wrong. Vocational education in a university context becomes inappropriate only when emphasis is shifted, for whatever reasons, from language to literature. The distinction between 'language' and 'literature' is that of Michael Oake-shott (1967, p. 308), who designates a language as a manner of thinking and a literature or a text as what has been said from time to time in a language. In a vocational education, what is studied is a literature or text, and not a language. What is being acquired is almost always a knowledge of what has been authoritatively said, rather than familiarity with the manner of thinking which has generated what has been said.

A similar point has been made by K. R. Minogue in *The Concept of a University* (1973, p. 94), in which he urges that the distinction between the practical and academic worlds is exemplified in the difference between a phrase book and a grammar book.

'Phrase books are quick and effective, and they are based upon what experience shows to be the most commonly used words and idioms. To master a phrase book is to learn a language after the manner in which a child learns it. And as this example shows, it is by no means the case that someone who has mastered a phrase book is limited to the mechanical repetition of phrases about the pen of my aunt and the demeanour of the coachman. A little ingenuity will generate an infinite number of further possible sentences out of the phrase book, according to the skill of the user. A grammar book, on the other hand, is an analysis of the language, and the fact that grammar is not central to speaking is shown by the fact that it is taught to children who already have a fluent mastery of their language. Thereby they learn not to do the right thing, but to know why it is the right thing. A grammar book begins, of course, as a description and analysis of an actually spoken language, but in time it comes to act as a criterion of how that language ought to be spoken.'

Clearly, it is possible for a technical subject to be taught as 'grammar', and Tait's analysis of the fascination of chemistry implies this sort of approach. Objections arise either when a subject degenerates into a mere accumulation of 'facts' with too little emphasis on explanatory concepts, or when the general cultural significance of the mode of thought is lost to sight. Derman Christopherson (1973, p. 44) made a similar point:

'Broadly speaking, a subject is an appropriate one for university study if its intellectual content and depth are sufficient to call for forms of learning and teaching in which the universities are expert, if its cultural, economic and social significance is, and will continue to be, such that it is desirable to attract to its study a proportion of the most able young people available, and, of course, if research has produced ideas and insights of such penetration and significance that their continuation and development must be assured.'

Dissatisfaction with professional education for failing to meet any one or any combination of the above major goals has led in the past to various attempts at compensation. The reasons for attempting compensatory education have varied interestingly in recent decades, and it is appropriate to review them briefly before examining the form in which the problem currently appears.

(c) *The principal aims and methods of compensatory education*
Holstein and McGrath (1960) distinguish in historical sequence between aims of compensatory education as follows: the aims of (1) gentlemanly cultivation; (2) mind training; (3) personal-business success; and (4) citizenship. The first of these, that of gentlemanly cultivation, is on the wane, not only because it was very difficult to decide what were the marks of a gentleman and what particular virtues were to be cultivated, but also because the notion of gentlemanly cultivation did more to put engineering teachers off liberal studies than it did to encourage their acceptance. There has also been a sneakingly Veblenesque fear of the 'cultural sheep-dip' designed to make the workers of this world look like the leisure class.

The second aim, that of mind training, has also been progressively on the retreat. The hope that there would be an automatic transfer of learning is now known to have been based on a theory of transfer far too naive to sustain a programme of humanities—or indeed of anything else.

The aim of education for business success still has some vitality. It can be detected in the recommendations of the Swann and Dainton committees. It also provides the reason for injecting into, for example, engineering degree courses studies in economics and industrial sociology. Those who criticise the concept of the technocracy claim that the injection of industrial sociology ('cow sociology' as it has derisively been called) is merely a cynical attempt to show engineers how to win friends and influence people, to manipulate the working class to maintain the power of the technocracy. Be that as it may, the demand for some form of social science education in professional education seems to grow daily and it is usually justified in terms of greater professional efficiency.

The fourth aim of compensatory education is in the ascendant at the time of writing—education for citizenship. This aim has been to develop a capacity and desire for public service in the professional and in the broader sense. The important subvariant form in which it currently appears is the aim of educating for social responsibility. The remainder of this chapter will be concerned with ways of realising these aims and with the important questions which are involved.

There are at least five approaches to the problem of producing among students engaged on professional training a developed sense of personal and social responsibility and a deeper and more comprehensive understanding of man's nature.(29)

The first approach is to assume that the problem does not exist, and to continue serenely with what is being done already.

The second approach is to add components to the professional discipline (usually with a sociological background) to evoke sensitivity to problems of social purpose and personal commitment. This technique, which will be called lateral enrichment in subsequent discussion, can readily incorporate teaching in the humanities—for example, by giving Shakespeare neat.

The third approach is to work outwards from the main discipline. This approach has been commended by Sir Eric Ashby in *Technology and the Academics* (1966, p. 48), in which he urges that the path to culture should be *through* a man's specialism, and not by circumventing it:

'Suppose a student decides to take up the study of brewing: his way to acquire general culture is not by diluting his brewing courses with popular lectures on architecture, social history, and ethics, but by making brewing the core of his studies. The *sine qua non* for a man who desires to be cultured is a deep and enduring enthusiasm to do one thing excellently. So there must first of all be an assurance that the student genuinely wants to make beer. From this it is a natural step to the study of biology, microbiology, and chemistry: all subjects which can be studied not as techniques to be practised but as ideas to be understood. As his studies gain momentum the student could, by skilful teaching, be made interested in the economics of marketing beer, in public houses, in their design, in architecture; or in the history of beer-drinking from the time of the early Egyptian inscriptions, and so in social history; or in the unhappy moral effects of drinking too much beer, and so in religion and ethics. A student who can weave his technology into the fabric of society can claim to have a liberal education; a student who cannot weave his technology into the fabric of society cannot claim even to be a good technologist.'

The fourth approach is through interdisciplinary experiments. For reasons which will be explored in chapter 5, such experiments have had a chequered history and cannot, at present, be claimed to have had much success at undergraduate level.

A fifth approach is for those who are responsible for the core of professional studies to trust that other agencies and forces inside the wider university community will take care of that other part of the educating process not catered for in the main discipline. It is hoped that students will look upon the extra-curricular activities of the community as preservers of their sanity, and there is a touching trust that some other groups inside the institution will aim to keep alive some concern for matters outside detailed technicalities. Occasionally, a benevolent administration will try to do this by arranging, with voluntary attendance, special lectures by eminent fizzers or 'fire men', or will patronise in one way or another any attempt of students to diversify their studies.

It need hardly be said that this fifth approach is little different from the first. To point gleefully to a chemist who plays the violin as vindication of the view that his education is in any way liberal, is to trivialise the problem beyond belief.

To return, then, to the two approaches which have been extensively tried out and which hold hope for the future. The first approach is that of lateral enrichment. Typically, this approach involves the injection of parallel studies drawn from the humanities and social sciences into the syllabus of the professional course. It could be argued that to study literature, history, philosophy, or any other of the humanities within the context of, say, engineering education is particularly valuable. For the training of the expert tends to emphasise information, whereas study of the humanities throws the emphasis rather onto consciousness, making a salutary redress of the balance.

The administrative conveniences of lateral enrichment are as attractive as the academic virtues. Lateral enrichment is tidy, inexpensive, and the least injurious or upsetting to the other parts of the system. It allows change to be felt and adjusted to in a gradual way. It allows every opportunity for ideas to be tried and tested and for change to occur when ineffectiveness in a particular area is known and widely accepted.(8)

But this very administrative convenience can be seen as the greatest weakness of the approach. Low cost is not in itself a commendation; cheapness is not a substitute for efficiency. The great danger with lateral enrichment is that the 'liberal studies' may have little effect on a student's general consciousness because they influence only a tiny part of his total culture. When students have rebelled against 'liberal studies' it has often been because they have not seen them as flowing out of their present predicament or being in any way related to their future role in society. Conversely, however, the desire to undertake studies outside the main discipline may stem from the student's realisation that his chosen profession has a general cultural significance which he must understand in order to operate effectively. In this case, work can become integrated and positive.

Whatever may be the many and varied benefits of study of the humanities as a way of enlarging consciousness, modest adjustments and alterations in a sub-system in the cause of lateral enrichment are likely to be inadequate as measures to expose the cultural basis of an entire profession. Indeed, the very subject-matter of the humanities may simply by-pass the central problems of social responsibility with which the students will be concerned. 'Man in Society' courses are not necessarily any better remedy, because in seeking to avoid the dangers of disciplinary parochialism they may restrict a student's freedom further by picking almost arbitrarily upon aspects of contemporary or earlier civilisation which may not engage a student's *personal* interest. The great attraction of the approach which works outwards from a specialism is that because the student has chosen the specialism, a central *core* of interest may be anticipated.

This is not to say that his chosen specialism will be his only interest. The Ashby approach could be extremely limiting by encouraging a student to see the world from only one point of view. Ashby's approach is also in danger of trivialising other studies by insisting on the emphasis of what may be minor concerns in major disciplines (for example, in ethics—the moral consequences of too much drinking) in the interests of thematic tidiness. A modified version of this approach may, however, be what is required, in which a student may see the relation of his knowledge to society.

The danger of professional education purely in a technical competence is that it does implicitly what Russian education is explicitly designed to do (equip a man to fulfil a specific niche in society), but without letting the student apprehend the social significance of his learning. Western educators, suspicious of a possible element of coercion in the Russian approach, sometimes overlook the limiting nature of our own modes of technical education. In similar manner, the danger of general education, seen as an accretion of knowledge which gives a cultivated veneer and a greater fluency or ease of association with those trained in other disciplines, is that the main discipline may never be critically evaluated.

The truly liberal education which alters a student's view of the nature of his expertise depends upon the training of his perceptions. If the social and ethical basis of a profession is to be understood, the fundamental need is for people to reflect more deeply on the social relationships in which they are set; the people who make them possible; the way power operates within them. To see the professional role for which one is preparing oneself as others see it may require some form of cultural migration.

(d) *Engagement-reflection patterns of study*

One way in which this sort of cultural migration has been achieved, is through what Anthony Dyson called 'an engagement–reflection pattern'.(8) Students at theological college, training for the priesthood, are intending professionals just as much as are students studying chemistry, engineering, or architecture. A pattern of study developed at Ripon Hall, Oxford, requires that a student spend a certain amount of time each week in a particular kind of church agency, or a social or community agency in which he is actually put to work in some way so that there he has a modest degree of responsibility during the time he is working. Every week, he has to complete a log and an evaluation sheet about his placement so that he develops a pattern of reflection on what he is doing. The questions asked in the evaluation sheet are linked with the work which he is doing in his programme of academic studies.

The aim of this programme of placements is to achieve a situation in which the theological student is not particularly conscious of being a theological student—where he is wrenched into a rather different world, a form of 'culture shock'. The process of 'clericalisation' sets in before a man is ordained and the aim of the Ripon Hall programme is to have him work in a set of social relationships and activities different from that of his intended professional role. Anthony Dyson has described the principles and practice of this scheme in detail in *Education and Social Action* (Goodlad, 1975).

Cultural migration of a comparable kind is known to be the advantage of voluntary service overseas or of periods of community service, and indeed of the sandwich principle widely used in technical education. The periods of engagement with practical problems raise fundamental questions about consensus, criteria of judgment, standards of value. The period of reflection provides the opportunity for review of the intellectual processes most suitable to their solution. When the commonest criticism of the 'academic' approach to human affairs is that it is discipline-oriented rather than goal-oriented, or problem-centred, there is a readily observable advantage in mingling the study of specific problems with the study of the intellectual principles which show that problems exist.

Such tactics for introducing the study of values into the education of intending professionals may be profoundly disturbing to both teachers and taught, and may dramatically challenge the nature of authority in professional education. It becomes difficult for the teacher to be seen as 'one who knows' when the coherence of a discipline is shown not to be intrinsic (concerned with specialised modes of thought), but extrinsic—temporarily arrived at, as it were, as a parallelogram of social forces in dynamic tension.

Education in values is relatively easy when these values are based on comfortable certainties of social order and cultural objective. But in a plural society no such certainties exist. The tension between manpower-planning goals of matching men to jobs, of 'consumer' goals of status and security, of individual goals of personal development, and of 'academic' goals for the elaboration of theory, can be immensely productive of educational benefit if it is recognised, acknowledged, and made the basis of explicit curricular action. Intending professionals, or experts, will be 'free', as opposed to 'trained', when they are invited to explore with their teachers the nature and purpose of their intended work, the economic and political forces which result in specific knowledge and skills being needed by society, the role strains set up by competing demands within a profession, the 'meaning' of the work for the individual—which may involve metaphysical questions—and the 'meaning' of the work in society at large (different from its economic and political necessity as immediately perceived). All of this will, inevitably, involve teleological questioning, as well as the theoretical knowledge and practical skills usually dealt with in the university. It need hardly be said that the education of the expert must include a strong component of the *known*, because the individual's sense of personal identity depends upon a feeling of mastery. If being 'cultured' involves having internalised the greatest possible number of features of one's 'culture', it is absolutely necessary in a plural society that the intending professional learn how to recognise and cope with uncertainty. He will never do this if he is led to believe that to become an expert he must just learn 'the facts'.

Again, there is a tension which must be maintained. Experts are 'people who know the answers'; education for uncertainty may thus be seen as potentially subversive. No doubt this is why lateral enrichment of professional studies is preferred to more radical forms of education in values. Critical evaluation of the knowledge deemed to be the property of a profession (and by implication of a university or polytechnic department preparing students for entry into that profession) is rightly seen as a challenge to authority.

CHAPTER FOUR

The Training of the Free

Does the authority generally accorded to the humanities, and thus the traditional claim of the humanities to take a major part in liberal education, stem from the intrinsic value and importance of the subject-matter of the various humanistic disciplines? Or does it rather stem from extrinsic attributes of these disciplines—the processes and modes of scholarship through which the subject-matter is handled?

One of the main values of any form of general education, as contrasted with training for a prescribed role, is to increase the individual's awareness of choice. General education is education in self-awareness, and self-awareness can, ideally, follow from the study of any of the major humanities or social sciences. For example, social anthropology can make one more sensitive to the special features of one's own society by contrast with the social institutions of other societies. History may sharpen a sense of significance in human behaviour. Philosophy, by the systematic demolition of incoherence, may aid the perception of intellectual coherence. Through knowledge of themselves, gained through such disciplines, people may become more sensitive to the uniqueness of others; by studying others, they may become more deeply aware of what they have in common with them. It is not difficult to see the value of such studies when linked to a central core of technical knowledge which gives a professional identity to an individual. But, how can one justify the full-time study of the humanities by undergraduates in universities? It is no answer to say that teachers of these subjects will be needed—for this is to put the question one stage further back. What is the justification for teaching the humanities in universities at all? Is the professed student of the humanities humanised as a matter of course? By no means. He —or she—runs one of two risks: dilettantism or pedantry. The element of training may be too weak, so that studies become trifling or self-indulgent; or else technique in the form of scholarly manoeuvres may be so arduous and seem so important as to mask almost entirely the human significance of the object of study. The problem within the humanities is to ensure that the training, that is, the disciplined scholarly study, is serious and demanding, while at the same time seeing that the student does not lose the capacity for direct encounter with literature, history, or philosophy, as embodiments of human experience.

Although every discipline in the humanities has its own way of imposing a framework of restricted intellectual perception on reality, this chapter is limited to a consideration of English in university studies and seeks to show by reference to it the advantages and disadvantages of humane studies.

F. R. Leavis claimed that English is a central discipline in the university and that literary criticism is central to the activity of an English school:

'The essential discipline of an English school is the literary-critical; it is a true discipline, only in an English school if anywhere would it be fostered, and it is irreplaceable. It trains, in a way no other discipline can, intelligence and sensibility together, cultivating a sensitiveness and precision of response and a delicate integrity of intelligence—intelligence that integrates as well as analyses and must have pertinacity and staying power as well as delicacy.' (Leavis, 1961, p. 34)

Since Leavis wrote those words, the study of literature in the university has become even more highly professionalised and the number of students reading English has increased dramatically. One wonders how long this 'essential discipline', of such an individual and refined character, can survive the techniques of mass production. In a system designed to supply the maximum number of 'consumers' with degree certificates with the greatest efficiency and despatch, emphasis is increasingly being thrown on standard techniques of analysis, textbook imitations of scholarly work. While the professional scholar may use critical apparatus as a means to an end, there is a danger that, in the rush for a degree qualification, students may become accomplished in exercises which are more important than the experience they deal with. 'Consumer' goals and 'academic' goals may be in conflict. Instruments can become ends. One cannot, of course, evaluate a trend in the development of a discipline without a fixed point of observation. For this reason, it is particularly important to ask whether the authority of English derives from its subject-matter or from the scholarly modes through which the subject-matter is analysed. Some of the virtues claimed for English studies concern subject-matter: some concern approach to subject-matter. To expose the authority of

English studies, each virtue claimed for those studies will be contrasted with a correlative weakness.

(a) *Judgment and evaluation v. following fashion*

First, it is claimed that English is uniquely concerned with judgment and evaluation. Denys Harding(13) argued that although the sciences must always imply or express some values, the humanities very often, and characteristically, deal directly with values—human evaluations—as part of their subject-matter. Acts of evaluating entail firstly, finding this or that thing interesting, and secondly (in reality simultaneously) liking or disliking it in some measure. These particular acts of attention and appraisal are organised as interests and as sentiments for ideals. Literature deals essentially in these evaluations. Each work of literature invites us to attend to something the writer has found interesting (and the discriminations he has made), and to agree with the attitudes (often a complex of attitudes) he implicitly expresses, or to agree with him about the difficulty of choosing among different shades of attitude. So too in history it is an important, if not essential, part of it that we examine situations that people and peoples have found themselves in, how they perceived them (that is, what discriminations they made), what attitudes they adopted, what actions they chose, and what the human outcome was. Theology, philosophy, legal studies, languages, psychology, social anthropology, geography, social sciences, are similarly dealing as part of their subject-matter with human evaluations. In science, by contrast, evaluations are *about* work, not part of it.

The pedagogical problem arises when one asks whether the evaluations integral to the work of creative writers should themselves be evaluated. Granted that every work of literature involves a criticism of the society in which the author lived and for which he wrote (a premise by no means everyone would accept), does it follow that the best practice for students is to judge, rather than to receive, the evaluations made by the writer? And if students are required to make judgments, by what standards are their judgments to be judged? Can a tutor's assessment of student criticism be anything other than ideological? Presumably, the only way in which a university teacher can evaluate a student's comments about a question of human evaluation is by whether or not he happens to agree with them; and is this to be the way in which his authority is revealed? If this seems a perverse and wilful simplification, it at least indicates that a teacher may find some difficulty in being objective about the judgments of his students.

The dilemma is not the only one which has to be confronted when one considers the teaching of criticism. For example, the explicit teaching of judgment, through constant 'marking' of authors and the habit of comparative practical criticism, is positively damaging.(14) The combination of criticism and analysis in the response to unseen passages seems likely to encourage premature formulation of judgment and the blur of double vision, and to inhibit empathy and wise passiveness. It can foster a habit of suspiciousness even in serious readers.

Inevitably, the practice of applying judgment to the human evaluations embodied in literature resolves itself into the question of whether those evaluations are 'good' or 'bad'. The inevitable confrontation with such a final form of judgment is both one of the strengths and one of the chief weaknesses of literary education.

The danger associated with judgment and evaluation is that of following fashion. Some teachers try to bridge the 'generation gap' by joining each generation of students in its current enthusiasms, literary, socio-political, or artistic. The importance of establishing a regard for high scholarly standards on the basis of personal acts of discrimination, liking, and preference (rather than lip service to the edicts of authority) has long been accepted, but teachers have only recently felt obliged to seek really close acquaintance with the momentary fashions of forms of writing. Such following of fashion is a devoted tactic at the university level, even a kind of martyrdom, because enthusiasms change fast.(13).

There are perhaps even more important reasons for being cautious than the rapid obsolescence of fashionable knowledge. Judgment and evaluation are subject to fashion in other ways. First, the subject-matter to which scholarly attention is devoted by students inevitably reflects the tastes and choices of those who selected the material. But the selectors may not be those with any educative purpose. There is obviously a world of difference between subject-matter selected systematically by scholars—to illustrate some perennial questions of morality, political economy, etc.—and the literature exciting critical attention in fashionable weeklies. The public visibility of some fiction —the James Bond sagas of Ian Fleming come immediately to mind— may be the result of commercial energy in which paperback books are sold like cans of beans rather than of any distinguishing virtue the book may have. Again, some books may provide a loose intellectual framework to sustain the social interaction of a youth cult. One suspects, for example, that the intrinsic interest of the writings of J. R. R. Tolkien or Herman Hesse is less important to their readers than the social interaction which knowledge of the contents of these books permits. If scholarly activity were to be devoted to evaluating the social values in such writings, the content of literary studies would be highly susceptible to the pressures of aggressive and resourceful publishers. Intellectual autonomy would go out of the window.

But if the subject-matter of books is susceptible to fashion, so also is the approach to it. Literature is a subject of central interest in the

humanities because it deals with human evaluations and is an econo-
mical way of access to human questions of perennial importance. It
is for precisely this reason that the mode of literary study is so responsive to intellectual fashions of the day. Syllabus architects and curriculum planners may be gravely tempted to direct students' attention
to 'good' literature defined through some social or other preoccupation which simply eliminates important imaginative work not favour-
able to a particular, or indeed to any, 'party line'. Drawing up the
agenda is an awesome responsibility. One solution to the problem is
simply to work and re-work a handful of authors whose writing has
became part of a syllabus by accident or by tradition—Jane Austen,
D. H. Lawrence, or Charles Dickens. On what 'authority' is one
work selected for a syllabus in preference to another?

(b) *Complexity and particularity v. fragmentation of culture*

It is in resisting the merely fashionable judgment and the too-easy
classifying of evaluation that the second major virtue of literary
studies is to be found. The appreciation of complexity through particularity is central in the humanities and in literature in particular.
The concern involved is with morality perceived through intelligence.

> 'The more advanced the work the more unmistakably is the judg-
> ment that is concerned inseparable from that profoundest sense of
> relative value which determines, or should determine, the im-
> portant choices of actual life.' (F. R. Leavis, 1961, p. 35)

It is not just that to understand all is to forgive all, but that to study
morality in some particular situation is to become sensitised to social
reality.

Concern with detail and particularity is a major virtue which the
humanities, and literature in particular, can claim over the social
sciences. In some disciplines, abstractions abound and grand theories
of society are bartered in bewilderment by students who do not understand the value of the intellectual currency which they are handling.
At best, the study of literature forces attention to specific social situations, from which one may work outward to social theories and unifying concepts. Without such a healthy emphasis on particularity, the
intellectual codification of experience can rapidly degenerate into
cliché. To know and value the particularity, passion, character, and
complexity of literature is to be able to know and criticise the stereotyped, simplified words and images of politicians, journalists, and
salesmen.(14)

Particularity, however, carries with it the correlative danger of
fragmentation of culture. Situation ethics have been criticised for failing to discriminate between situations of major qualitative difference.

In like manner, particularity, uninformed by general theories and concepts unifying one sector of experience with another, can be bewildering. The strength and weakness of some social science theorising is conceptual density. The humanities can claim to offer indispensable intellectual roughage. But there is a danger that the humanities will be perceived as *nothing but* roughage. There is obviously a danger that an otherwise valuable and virtuous attention to detail in studying, for example, a specific literary text, may be rendered sterile by inadequate contact with a programme of observation of greater scope.

Another danger concerning the fragmentation of culture may arise both from the interest in complexity through particularity and from a careful attempt to avoid following fashion. If academic study in English is conceived without any reference at all to contemporary student culture, and if particular concern is paid to works of literature whose cultural significance is not made clear, students may well compartmentalise their cultural life. Sensitive and scholarly studies of arcane and ancient detail may be put in one compartment ('work'), while a more spontaneous, uncritical, yet not less sensitive response to contemporary literature is put into another compartment ('recreation'). It follows that, just as curriculum planners need to be explicit about the human evaluations which they put in front of students, so must teachers, anxious to communicate a love for both particularity and complexity, be explicit about the relative values of particularity and of synthesising concepts.

(c) *New perceptions v. secondhandness*

The third major virtue claimed for a literary education is that it involves a student in new perceptions. In Barbara Hardy's words, a literary education is not the induction into something alien, but an invitation to look more intelligently, consciously, formally, and imaginatively at the stories we tell, the feelings we experience, the roles we play and impose, the jokes and satires we make, the symbols we need, and the historic sense we grope after. A literary education, she urged, is not guaranteed to make us more active or unselfish, but is certainly able to make life more conscious and complicated.(14) The better literature at all levels (including film, popular song, detective and science fiction stories, and television) has the effect, in whatever degree, of dislocating momentarily one's own vision of experience, one's own painfully achieved order, then of compelling a clarification and a re-adjustment of that order in response to the work being examined.(3)

It could be said of any discipline that it involves its students in new perceptions. The uniqueness of Copernicus, as Polanyi has pointed out, was in his shifting the location of the imagined cosmic observer from the earth to the sun—a grand act of intellectual audacity. Literary criticism can, however, claim distinction as a particularly fertile form of consciousness. Not only is the material to which it is applied rich in unusual perceptions of the world, but the selective attention to detail within those perceptions which is imposed by the discipline of literary criticism can be peculiarly evocative—and singularly disturbing.

Perhaps it is because new perceptions are disturbing, and also difficult to achieve, that the correlative danger of secondhandness is one of the most serious in literary education. Secondhandness, it should be noted, is the outcome not of excess but of defect—of timidity rather than rashness. Barbara Hardy recalled how in drawing up a study scheme for a new examination in practical criticism for the University of London, she and her colleagues found it necessary to state formally that students would not be asked to pass value judgments on the literary passages that make up the paper.

'This statement may well strike colleagues in other universities as bizarre, and many of us felt doubtful both about the intent and the warning. The evaluation of literature has seemed to many critics, past and present, to be central to their subject. But those who supported the warning were moved by depressing experiences of stereotyped, imitated, non-personal and unargued critical judgments, and if there is anything more disheartening than imitation of analysis, it is surely the imitation of judgment.'(14)

The difficulty is a serious one. While literature may be seen to provide the most fertile source of new perceptions, the formal study of literature at university may seem to consist of no more than the sophisticated, unfeeling, and joyless regurgitation of predigested judgment. Academic exercises that elicit predictable responses give students no experience at all either of the intrinsic authority which content may command or of the extrinsic authority of scholarly enterprise. Such exercises simply expose them to the institutional authority of the examination hall—and if that is all that literary education has to offer, it does not matter very much what is studied nor how it is studied. In resolving this difficulty, the teaching style may be of critical importance. The more teaching is standardised, the more open it is to abuse: 'If there's a system, there's a racket to beat it!' Possibly the only antidote to secondhandness is a one-to-one regular contact between tutor and student; but even that can turn into a joint conspiracy against the examiner.

(d) *Disinterestedness v. over-specialisation*

Denys Harding argued that to distinguish university work as it should be from the exercises of equally high intelligence for the practical ends of industry, commerce, and administration, we have to add that it is disinterested—not calculatedly useless, but viewed as worth pursuing even if no practical use and no advantage, or only minimal advantage, in terms of money and career can be expected.

'What I see as proper to university work . . . is a high level of intelligence exercised disinterestedly along developed lines of concern for particular sorts of material, with sensitive responsiveness and fine discriminations in these directions, and with advanced and tested techniques and methods of discipline, the whole enterprise going on within a framework of values which is constantly being examined, probed and modified, especially by the humanities.'(13)

Harding acknowledged that only a small number of people will want to go far in this sort of programme. The majority of undergraduates see their courses as vocational preparation, leading either to a particular career (architecture, dentistry, etc.) or to a fairly broad range of employments (in one of the sciences, for instance, or administration). But, he suggested, it is the nucleus of academics who try disinterestedly to reach the highest standards they can in the humanities or the sciences that makes the university something other than a cluster of training centres.

The disinterested pursuit of high scientific standards may receive public support (from businessmen, politicians, and public administrators) because disinterested work in the sciences may unpredictably turn out to have the practical applications that industry and administration appreciate. No such manifest applicability justifies support of the humanities. In universities that have both arts and science faculties there is still a tendency for the humanities to get carried along in the sciences' financial slipstream. Perhaps more important though less tangible, a persisting feeling can be detected that it would somehow be a bad thing not to have a small number of dedicated scholars in society (a residual superstition which still contributes to the continued support of the humanities). The better chance of survival for the humanities depends, however, not on a 'financial slipstream' nor on this residual superstition, but on something intrinsic to the relation between the nucleus of scholars and the large number of students who dimly respect high scholarship even while regarding it as an eccentricity.

'Of course it is eccentric, but only through having carried to a high level a kind of activity that very large numbers of people find satisfying in simpler forms. An elementary interest in history, psychology, literature, the arts, even philosophy, besides politics, economics and science, can all be found in a popular newspaper. The rudiments of an interest in most branches of the humanities are part of any ordinary child's intellectual life, and by the end of the school years we have been at least on the nursery slopes of a good many disciplines that reach their peak in the best university work. More than anything else it is the genuine continuity between academic pursuits and everyday interest that most hopefully promises the survival of high standards, just as the enthusiasm for high achievement in games and athletics depends on our familiarity with lower levels of the same kinds of skill.'(13)

Harding suggested that the glimpsing of high standards was probably the prime benefit of non-vocational university education.

The concept of disinterestedness is such an important one in university education that it is examined in detail in Chapter 7. Suffice it to note at this point that the disinterested pursuit of high standards is a virtue extrinsic to the subject-matter of any particular discipline, such as English. It is also a highly fragile virtue and can easily lead to the correlative danger of over-specialisation. If a subject is studied without reference to a society wider than that of the scholar's immediate colleagues, there is a danger that his preoccupations become more and more remote from the concerns of ordinary men. Consequently, the fruits of his scholarship will become less and less interesting and less and less accessible to those who should benefit from his study. The widespread observation that a scholar's university responsibilities for teaching and for research pull in different directions is testimony to this. The needs of undergraduates for closer contact with high standards through ready interaction with scholars disinterestedly pursuing knowledge may become impossible if the scholar's 'research' is in some remote and inaccessible area of knowledge.

The balance of considerations is a delicate one. If, in an attempt to avoid over-specialisation, scholarship has too *strong* a social reference, the quality of disinterestedness is easily corrupted.

(e) *Exact scholarship v. academicism*

The fifth major virtue of study in English is that it involves exact scholarship and disciplined study. Harding suggested that the conventional contrast between the sciences and the arts is not the right one for all purposes: in some ways the important contrast is that between, on the one hand, creative work in the arts, appreciation of the arts, and those aspects of the humanities in which human values form the subject-matter for close attention and systematic discussion —and, on the other, science and the disciplinary aspects of the humanities. The scholar engaged in the intellectual dissection of a problem in the humanities adheres to ideals of exact definition, specialised knowledge, concern with factual evidence and logical rigour that bring him closer in spirit to the scientist; his work, moreover, may be as unconcerned as the scientist's with values other than the scrupulous exercise of intelligence in a specialised field.

'I remember a college scholarship committee which was having to make research grants to both arts and science candidates. A broad-minded physicist, well disposed to the arts faculty, agreed readily to a grant for an intensive study of the linguistic features of eleven lines from the *Ancrene Riwle*, but a proposed enquiry into the influence of the short story form on D. H. Lawrence's work struck him as not being research at all but simply critical opinion which might deserve to be expressed but should not be supported from research funds. The Lawrence study was the more likely to bear on the evaluative aspects of the humanities, but the ideals that most obviously link the humanities to the sciences were to be found in the exact technical scholarship required for the *Ancrene Riwle*.

This kind of exact scholarship might seem to offer a potential bridging point, allied in spirit with the sciences, but also having close relations with the value aspects of creative work, of cultures, and of periods. But the relation between scholarship and evaluation is too often ineffective; even when the two sides are united in one person—a good editor and a sensitive critic—they are not always brought into rewarding contact, but the man exercises first one side of himself and then the other. It sometimes seems as though this gap is as hard to span as that between humanities and sciences. It is not often focused as a problem needing a cooperative solution, though there is too often underlying tension and occasional open hostility between the two sides, perhaps especially between scholars and critics in literature.

A better understanding of the relation of these two aspects might contribute to making the values represented by the humanities more accessible to scientists.'(13)

It is difficult to know quite what to make of the example given, which seems to carry the extraordinary message that pedantry is a valuable interdisciplinary and integrating principle—a liberal suggestion which is enough to send one posting back to the *trivium* and *quadrivium*. Harding is right, however, in saying that the gap between scholar and critic is often as hard to bridge as that between sciences and humanities, and that a better understanding of the relation of scholarship and criticism might make the values represented by the humanities more accessible to scientists. When scientists and technologists feel they want something from the arts subjects, as many do, it is surely the disciplined and sensitive presentation of human values, or the disciplined and developed enjoyment of the perceptual arts, that they want. They have to be shown that there is a respectworthy discipline even in the evaluative aspects of the humanities.

Though the authority of a discipline in the humanities such as English may be revealed to those most sceptical through exact scholarship and disciplined study, there is again a correlative danger, this time of academicism, which may utterly destroy the authority of the discipline. Scholarship, the tough, grinding minutiae that make up 'academic excellence', is of the essence of what a university stands for. There are no short cuts. The scholar who fudges his results or argues dishonestly because of a further good is in deep trouble—and we all know it. Contrariwise, the scholar who exalts minutiae to the point where they have ceased to be a means and have become an end beyond which he will not look is an object of pity.(27b) Barbara Hardy noted that the formal analysis of styles and structure may obscure that very sense of passion and particularity which is the nerve of literary response.

> 'So much of the technique of analysis has been passed on without the sensibility (compare the wit, tentativeness, irony, and feeling of Empsom with an imitation analysis of ambiguity) that we can find essays, articles, theses, books, and, alas, teachers, who analyse the form without the spirit, understanding the individuality of poems and authors while exaggerating the difference between authors and readers.'(14)

At least one consequence of such impersonalising of literary criticism has been a retreat from form to subject-matter. The emphasis on theme rebukes the analysts, insists on the link between life and literature, the experience of reader and the experience of artist and creates a very useful means of relating different disciplines.

The paradox, and the danger for university pedagogy, is that the very virtues of exact scholarship and disciplined study which give such subjects as English their intellectual authority may be at the same time a source of their undoing. How may one preserve the study of English as an autonomous intellectual discipline commanding respect for its specialised intellectual procedures, yet at the same time offering general education both to its specialist students themselves and also to those who are never going in their professional lives to use those intellectual procedures?

It is not as if educators were assisted by pervasive respect, in society at large, for either the man of letters or the prophet. Poets are neither acknowledged nor unacknowledged legislators, and will only invite ridicule if they draw their singing robes about them. Seymour Betsky(3b) offered a diagnosis of the 'inaccessible malaise' afflicting the discipline of Letters. We do not know whether serious Letters exemplifying standards has a sense of function within industrial culture.

Is the discipline alive or dead, or only guardian of a vast museum? He drew attention to three aspects of Letters today: as a commodity in a consumer-oriented culture; as a form of communication; and as imaginative literature. As a *commodity*, serious literature has little market value. The public does not wish to examine closely a presented way of life. Its principal goal is to enjoy decent living standards, in the achieving of which people quite other than writers bear major responsibility: first, those directly involved in the process—that is, a large national leadership associated with production, distribution, and manipulating consumption, as well as a Government leadership concerned to encourage its efforts; next, educated manpower—that is, scientists, technologists, economists, many political scientists, sociologists, psychologists, and the like; thirdly, those concerned with the democratic process in industrialism—which they interpret as the greatest happiness of the greatest number; last, a national leadership concerned with 'communications' of all kinds and at all levels. As *communication*, serious Letters has to compete with other forms: these today are, in overwhelming numbers, practical, or technical, or persuasive. As *imaginative literature*, it is in competition with a multi-billion-dollar industry of escape, wish-fulfilment, distraction, entertainment; indulgence in sexual possibility to compensate for what has gone wrong in the world of personal relations; indulgence in violence and crime as an outlet for frustrations and angers triggered by the culture; a literature marked by sentimentality, simplification, melodrama.

Yet, a large number of serious writers exists. But each—while offering highly crafted product in a culture geared to standardised 'formula' products—has to compete against the other for recognition, status, and a living wage. It is important to gain a just estimate of the present situation of the writer and critic. We ought to realise that, in our day at least, no disproportionate burden of responsibility may be placed on writer or critic as a significant influence in our culture. By the early nineteenth century, the writer was beginning, but only beginning, to be aware of the kinds of phenomenon that we now feel to be overwhelming. Today, the position and function of the writer within an industrial culture is felt by the industrialist to be somewhat irrelevant; by the scientist to be unreliable; by the labour movement —the people interested in democracy—to have little to contribute to the solution of the tough problems we have to face. Writers and critics suffer almost intolerable pressures which derive from their uncertainty about a sense of function. They waste time and energy when they criticise one another. Far better to cooperate in the common pursuit.

If literary studies, with the highly crafted works which form their subject-matter, are of little cultural significance nowadays, there are important implications for the 'training' of the free—for disciplined education in the humanities. The study of English in the university has been criticised in the past as being one more example of the self-indulgence of the leisured class. In some universities its content was to a disproportionate extent the written record of upper-class life, and its pedagogic mode 'belles-lettres-istic chatter'.(19) The powerful movement initiated by Richards and Leavis, involving concentration in schools and universities on close reading, was a welcome and necessary corrective to this chatter; but it is now inhibiting the wide and ranging reading which it should be one of the purposes of education in the humanities to foster.

There is a further danger, perhaps particularly likely to arise in an egalitarian educational system. I have seen a 'students' text' of Shakespeare's *Twelfth Night*—a monstrous volume in both concept and physical size—containing the text of Shakespeare's play, reams of editorial chit chat—and specimen answer-essays written by 'professors' to every conceivable examination question about the play. If such elaborate techniques are exercised on elegant trivia, the result is even worse. A literature which may have had a spurious currency as material for salon gossip becomes utterly debased when filtered through the triple screen of scholarly commentary, textbook digest of scholarly commentary, and student-essay-digest-of-textbook-digest-of-scholarly-commentary.

There are large numbers of students whose interest is not in scholarship but in a degree certificate. One must hope that this very practical interest can be turned by their teachers to the account of genuine education. But how is this best done, as far as English is concerned? Moreover, if such students are the majority, there is also a minority of potential scholars. If scholarship in English is to survive as a valuable element of modern culture, their powers must be preserved and trained. Should there, then, be a division of syllabus and emphasis with something diluted, less demanding in both content and treatment, provided for those whose interest is in reading but not in scholarship? This would be dangerous. The work of such students would be robbed of its seriousness. For them, 'chatter' might be approved and intensified, while the chosen scholars pursued their austere and dedicated way. Perhaps the use of scholarly techniques with some degree of severity should normally be a postgraduate enterprise. Lionel Knights quoted Wordsworth's view that the proper calling of youth is to 'accumulate in genial confidence'. Perhaps all undergraduates should spend most of their time reading in this spirit, often meeting the demands of great and difficult works and gradually mastering the principles of critical method, but without being pressed to use the minutiae of scholarship. Perhaps, too, English should not constitute the whole of an undergraduate course.

If literature is only part of modern culture, although a very concentrated and fertile part, it could be argued that it should be seen in its setting. A work of literature may offer a unique form of perception, exposure to some radically new insight, or the deepening of traditional insight through transforming consciousness. But, in the last analysis, how do we know that a particular literary perception is worth noting? The problem is not a new one in scholarship: was, for example, *Pearl* a typical or exceptional mediaeval poem? Is Steinbeck's story *The Pearl* a typical or exceptional twentieth-century cultural product? The scholarly apparatus of English studies may aid perception, may facilitate choice of literary excellence by helping the common reader to detect stylistic or logical flaws in a work of art. But the intrinsic authority of many works of art, their intellectual and emotion appeal, often transcends detail. How old was Hamlet? How many children had Lady Macbeth? Who cares? Scholarship and criticism may, for the common reader, be like the scaffolds cradling a ship before launching—readily and necessarily discarded as the ship floats away. Other forms of preoccupation in English studies may be similarly disposable. Indeed, if one removes the clutter of literary history, pseudo-Freudian hunt-the-symbol, structuralist conjurings, etc., what is left of the discipline?

Perhaps, then, the intrinsic authority of works of literature, the extrinsic authority of the modes of scholarship involved in English studies, and the educational potential of both taken in combination would be greatly enhanced if literature were never to be regarded as a subject for study on its own. It should perhaps find its place within the context of another 'subject' which takes a broader view of society— history, sociology, regional studies, etc.

Joint-honours degrees are not, of course, a panacea; nor is 'lateral enrichment' likely to be of any greater value in the education of humanists than it is in the education of intending professionals. For purposes of general humane education, 'The Training of the Free', it may be necessary to invent a totally new 'discipline'. The grouping of scholarly techniques and preoccupations which goes into an English school is not necessarily specific to given subject-matter. Literary criticism may be applied to anything written; so too may linguistic and historical aspects of scholarship. It must also be remembered that first-class writing can be encountered within the bounds of many great disciplines, science as well as arts. In short, an English school—or for that matter any other disciplinary grouping—may be seen as primarily a social, rather than an intellectual, phenomenon. And it may be from its social power as much as from its scholarly preoccupations that its authority derives.

What, then, characterises a discipline?

CHAPTER FIVE

What is a Discipline?

> 'First come I : my name is Jowett.
> There's no knowledge but I know it.
> I am Master of this college :
> What I don't know isn't knowledge.'

Authority in higher education has so far been discussed as though it were intrinsic to various types of specifically intellectual activity. The purpose of this chapter is to argue that a discipline is as much a social phenomenon as an intellectual one. In saying this, one runs the risk of stating the obvious: but heroic attempts at interdisciplinary manipulation have failed because inadequate attention has been paid to this fact.

In Archambault's collection of essays, *Philosophical Analysis and Education* (1965), Paul Hirst distinguishes between 'forms' and 'fields' of knowledge. The primary 'forms' are, he says, mathematics, physical sciences, human sciences, history, religion, literature and the fine arts, and philosophy. These forms must be learnt, at least in part, from a master on the job. The learning involves high critical standards, complex criteria, and a return from theory to experience. Hence they are properly called disciplines. It is its dependence on some particular kind of test against experience that distinguishes each major discipline from the others.

'Fields' are organisations of knowledge which are not themselves disciplines or sub-divisions of disciplines. They build, around specific objects, phenomena, or practical pursuits, knowledge which is rooted in more than one discipline. They are held together simply by their subject-matter. Geography is an example of a 'field' and so, by definition, is not a discipline. However, while a careful limitation such as Hirst's is appropriate in certain educational and philosophical contexts, there is no doubt that the word is often used more broadly, yet still responsibly, in higher education. The geography professor will not hesitate to refer to his subject as a discipline. It is difficult to find a synonym: 'subject' will not quite do, and 'field' could be ambiguous. The average academic would feel that he knew a discipline when he saw one, though he might be hard put to it to give an exclusive definition. He would expect it to have a coherent, though complex, body of subject-matter and skills, studied at a high intellectual level, and to possess a distinguishing theoretical structure. He would probably expect the work to contain an element of 'discipleship'—to be, in fact, 'learnt from a master on the job'.

In discussing the question 'What is a discipline?', I concentrate on ways in which property rights in knowledge impede or aid attempts to introduce questions of value into the professional education of experts, and correspondingly impede or aid attempts to show the social relevance of study of the humanities. I will argue that a discipline has vitality when it is neither divorced from nor wholly dependent upon education of students for a role in society, but is, rather, *related* to some aspects of social living. I start by discussing a discipline, theology, which is nowadays under some pressure in universities; I end by 'inventing' a discipline, showing what social manipulation would be required for its establishment.

(a) *The interpenetration of disciplines*

Theology is of interest not only because it is a humanistic discipline traditionally studied for a vocational purpose, but, more importantly, because its present status as a university discipline is threatened. It is faced with the challenge that it may no longer plausibly claim that status in its own right, because it can be reduced without remainder to other disciplines, once its children and now its more thriving neighbours—philosophy, literature, psychology, sociology. How do you teach theology when it is no longer assumed culturally that its subject-matter can be taken for granted? But though the dominance implied in the old title 'Queen of the sciences' is today neither possible nor desired, that title embodied an important principle—that theology is intimately concerned with every aspect of human knowledge. The present significance of theology in the university is not as the central pivot which organises, but as a place where pressure is felt; and it cannot do its own work without being in some relation to other disciplines.(5)

Christianity's function in modern Western society is catalytic rather than dominating. If theology is not to remain dead and neglected, it has perhaps need of three things: a university setting, lay participation, and the ecumenical dialogue—that is to say, contextual relevance. The conceptions of theologians are effective only if they are successfully 'aimed' at experience; and 'aiming' is an interdisciplinary business, which theologians undertake on their own at their peril. A symposium on the priesthood convinced Coulson that even questions of church order have to be argued out to the satisfaction of sociologists and psychologists. It is the questions posed from within another discipline that provoke theologians to develop and modify their assumptions. Any university department of theology which continued to cater exclusively for the declining number of ordinands would soon be out of business. How, then, can it be justified as a discipline in its own right against those disciplines which may claim to have superseded it? If we can justify the place of theology in a university, it may be that we shall have succeeded in showing what its function is within the culture of a plural society. This implies that the description of the discipline called 'theology' will be arrived at, to an important extent, on the university's terms and not its own.

Under contemporary pressures, the study of theology has been modified in some universities to become the study of religion. The emphasis, that is, has moved from the *theological* to the *descriptive*. In a paper on 'The place of religious studies in the humanities and social sciences'(31) Ninian Smart suggested that this study of religion needs to have four distinguishing marks: it must be plural, polymethodic, aspectual, and non-finite. It must be *plural*, because there are many traditions which need to be examined in both the Christian religion and others. It must be *polymethodic*, because several disciplines are needed for the study of religion and religions: for example, history, philology, sociology, and psychology. It must be *aspectual*, because the study of religion concentrates upon the treatment of religion as an aspect of human life. In this last respect it resembles the study of politics: the study of politics deals with the political behaviour and feelings as does that of religion with religious behaviour and feelings. Both politics and religion are in an important sense all-pervading; but they can also be studied aspectually. Last, the study of religion must be *non-finite*, because the boundaries of religion are not to be closely defined. Where does religion end and ideology begin? Ideologies not only play, very often, in the same league as religion: as Maoism shows, they also begin to exhibit religious-style behaviour. Such descriptive study—plural, polymethodic, aspectual and non-finite—is essentially humanistic, involving as it does empathy with the feelings and intentions of the adherents. There is a marked distinction between descriptive studies and those which are directly engaged in the questions of the truth and value of a religious faith or position.

It is important for the purpose of this chapter to see how religious studies relate to the humanities and the social sciences. The first form of relationship shown by Smart is that of overlap within this polymethodic discipline. The history of Christendom is part of the history of Western culture; the history of Christian art is part of the history of Western art; the sociology of religion is an aspect of sociology—

and so on. Another form of integration is achieved through philosophy. Christian doctrines themselves need philosophical scrutiny, and through such scrutiny are related to various aspects of modern knowledge—particularly scientific knowledge. Since, also, religious responses are deep and serious, and therefore can command the respect of those who are looking for a solution of existential problems, philosophical enquiries can be enriched by being related to religious systems. In addition, because of the ambiguities created by the existential nature of religious commitment (ambiguities of how far religious claims are objective and how far symbolic), there are ways in which the study of religion can connect with literature and the arts, which also to some extent explore existential aspects of human life.

Nor are the interdisciplinary possibilities perceived only from one side. Psychiatry could be taught to theological and medical students together. When a person says 'I'm the most wicked person in the world: God has turned his back on me', the psychiatrist says 'Endogenous depressive psychosis—marked self-reproach'. But theological students would be concerned at a different level, and would want to know other things about the patient. Does psychiatry or theology offer the more authoritative description of the patient's condition?(38) Proposals such as this are positive and promising. Nevertheless, so deeply engrained is departmentalism in the academic structure, and so much identified with status, that any close association between disciplines is seen partly as a love match and partly as a takeover bid. Even psychiatry, which at times has seemed to threaten theology, is itself threatened by such studies as physiology and psychopharmacology. Smart's notion of religious studies as a 'pervasive' subject is interesting and fruitful: religion must form part of the subject-matter for students of history, literature, sociology, psychology, philosophy and so on. But Smart had no doubt that religious studies needed its own power base in an institution—that is, a department.

As intellectual imperialists gaze greedily at the map of knowledge seeking where to plant flags, scholars need to gather together for mutual support. Boundaries, particularly in new disciplines, are maintained with all the fierceness of the territorial imperative. The struggle is sometimes exhilarating, sometimes depressing. Whichever way it is, the tension is bad for the development of that kind of insight into a discipline which comes by informal rather than formal means. For example, one may get the 'feel' of science more truly through everyday contact with scientific colleagues or fellow-students than from the apparently limitless success of their intellectual enterprise. One may hear something of the long-drawn-out tedium of research, the disappointments, the frustration from apparatus that will not do what it should, the delay in getting materials, the bafflement when they appear to be mysteriously contaminated, or when animals die or will not breed, and the elation from the occasional success. Such learning grows better in an atmosphere of relaxed cooperation than in one of anxious rivalry.(13)

(b) *The conflict of thought and action in traditional disciplines*
Departmental rivalries are not the only kind of conflict generated by the conventional system of university disciplines. The very nature of a discipline, as traditionally conceived, may cause tensions between the aims of a university and those of society. A common complaint about universities is that they are ill-adapted to deal with society's many pressing problems. The theoretical preoccupations of academics may be conducive to long-term understanding of complex interrelationships: the desires of society may be for the immediate solution of technical, social, psychological and other problems. The university is discipline-oriented: problems are defined within the perspective of a discipline, and solved—or, more often, endlessly refined—within the discipline. Practical problems may require approaches from a variety of disciplines simultaneously. K. R. Minogue (1973, pp. 99–100) distinguishes between practical and academic problems, arguing that the solution of one is not necessarily a solution of the others:

'Medically, the problem of cancer is two problems: a practical problem because we all want to cure the thousands who die of the disease, and a medical problem—or, rather, cluster of problems—about the behaviour of cells. It happens in this case that a solution to the academic problem may be a pre-condition of a solution to the practical problem: at least, this is a plausible way of looking at it. It might happen, of course, that someone might stumble across the cure for cancer, highly effective but quite mysterious. Or research might discover an explanation that did not help in curing. In the case of the cure without understanding, the practical problem would virtually have ceased, except perhaps for a certain amount of residual anxiety that the cures might merely be flukes, and that until the academic problem had been solved—i.e., until doctors had worked out some idea of *why* the cure was a cure—then there would be a considerable possibility of relapse.'

Minogue considers it an essential condition of the maintenance of the academic world that it retain a certain remoteness of academic from practical concerns. The academic approach to knowledge undoubtedly involves a form of perception which many people regard as a kind of distortion. It is precisely for this reason that the conflict of goals discussed in Chapter 2—in this case between the 'manpower' goal of supplying competent technicians to cope with society's illnesses, and the 'academic' goal of the elaboration of theory—reveals itself as one of the places where authority needs to be understood.

A large teaching hospital very often has three objectives—to cure sick people, to teach undergraduates, and to carry out research. Clearly, these objectives can be in conflict with one another. Medical students who are being taught by research-oriented doctors may develop a stronger interest in diseased organs than in people. Somewhat similarly, a university department of aeronautical engineering is likely to produce graduates who are interested in the technicalities of supersonic flight, regardless of whether supersonic flight is socially desirable. It is one of the perennial paradoxes of the academic world that the theoretical interest of academics very often stems directly from urgent practical concerns; yet at the same time the theoretical preoccupations may take on a life of their own, resulting in a conflict between the desire for understanding and the call for action. Correspondingly, it may be argued that the specific form of a theoretical preoccupation in a subject apparently removed from immediate practice owes more than the practitioners of the discipline would admit to practical concerns. For example, Gouldner (1971, pp. 125–34) has argued that the theoretical orientation of British anthropology derives from the needs of British colonial administration:

'The task of colonial administrators was not to facilitate change but to keep things stable and orderly. They wanted to do this with the smallest investment in state apparatus and the least cost of policing and administration. The colonies, after all, were not meant to be run at a loss. English administrators therefore wanted and welcomed a native social system that was orderly and self-maintaining, and Anthropological Functionalism, which was concerned with these problems, was relevant and congenial.' (p. 131)

Such sociological analysis of the genesis of the form of a theory does not, of course, in any way undermine the intellectual coherence or validity of that theory. Its value is to point to the important relationship between social groupings and intellectual preoccupations. Anyone inside or outside a university who wishes to see a reorientation of theoretical interest must pay as much attention to the social organisation of the learning and teaching as to its intellectual content.

(c) *The problem of planning interdisciplinary work*
In his essay 'On the classification and framing of educational knowledge' (Young, 1971, chapter 2), Basil Bernstein argues that in the 'collection' code of the traditional curriculum in English education, the emphasis is on states of knowledge. The contents of the subjects studied are clearly bounded and insulated from each other, and subject-loyalty is systematically developed in students. By contrast, in

an 'integrated' code, pedagogy is likely to emphasise ways of knowing rather than states of knowledge, and a synthesising and subordinating idea blurs boundaries between subjects.

The process of socialisation into 'collection' codes has been so strong in British education that, without a vigorous social structure to sustain an integrating idea, participants in interdisciplinary experiments are likely after a short while to wander back to the specialisms which gave them their professional identities. The difficulty of getting British university teachers to teach anything outside their specialisms is notorious. Moreover, if a department begins to ask value-questions, it may be experiencing a dangerous lack of faith. To raise such questions as 'What is chemistry for?' or 'Why are we studying chemistry at all?' may put severe doubts into the minds of students (to say nothing of their teachers). A Head of Department who wishes students to acquire some knowledge of economics, management, or even of subjects from the humanities and social sciences which would deepen personal understanding yet not necessarily enhance professional competence, runs a risk of weakening the administrative and social structure which sustains confidence in the subject as currently taught. Rather than permit outsiders to weaken the socialisation of his students, he may prefer to appoint his own mathematicians, economists, management experts, and even humanists. But he will inevitably experience difficulty in finding suitable people, not least because of salary and promotion structure.

Interdisciplinary courses are often in practice multidisciplinary. The degree of synthesis—the extent to which the relationship between all the component parts of a new course in the university or in a polytechnic is eventually apparent to the students and is a positive contribution to each of the separate parts—is determined by the people involved, much more often than by the name or theoretical structure of the course. Genuine integration of states of knowledge is extremely difficult to achieve.

The alternative to constructing courses around states of knowledge is to emphasise ways of knowing. One may distinguish several major types of knowing—scientific, moral, aesthetic, historical, religious and so on—which correspond closely with the 'forms' identified by Hirst. A way of knowing consists of a methodology and a perspective—a way of seeing an area of knowledge as being of particular importance in the whole field of knowledge. There is no reason at all why the methodology and perspective of one way of knowing should not be applied to the subject-matter or content of another. Indeed, an effective way of establishing an integrated, interdisciplinary approach to learning is teacher-based.

Chapter 3 discussed strategies for introducing considerations of value into the education of intending professionals. Chemistry, for example, may be considered to be one of the areas where content is most firmly fixed and where, although a distinctive way of knowing is involved, states of knowledge are the end-product of the educational enterprise. To shift the emphasis from states of knowledge to ways of knowing, it might seem most suitable to appoint staff specifically to explore, through teaching, the ways of knowing characteristic of the main discipline, and to show the links with ways of knowing characteristic of other disciplines—particularly those which would show the social relevance of the subject. But, how would such highly skilled teachers compare with researchers in their chance of getting promotion?

At present, kudos and 'international visibility' depend upon research and upon teaching at honours and if possible at postgraduate level. 'Publish or perish' is an all too well-worn cliché. As Caplow and McGee (1958) perceptively observed, the emphasis on research makes a man more interested in the job he is aiming to get than the job he is currently doing. This is an overstatement which does less than justice to the motivation of many university teachers. While these men and women may have their share of ambition, they often desire even more the increased facilities of a more senior post, and the chance to receive stimulus and inspiration through contact with a wider circle of scholars. But, however that may be, and whatever the wider social objectives of a university, it is clearly absurd that its teaching function should be severely weakened by the preoccupation of its faculty with the international structure of their discipline as opposed to the institutional needs of the university which is their home. Nevertheless, it seems improbable that a new breed of teacher dons could ever achieve the prestige of the researchers. Some different solution is required.

(d) *An 'interdisciplinary' discipline*

To illustrate these points about the intellectual and social characteristics of a discipline, and also to suggest tentatively a way of uniting the technical/professional studies and the humanities discussed in chapters 2 and 3, I offer the following description of a hypothetical 'discipline', one which is invented for the purposes of the present chapter. After outlining the theoretical framework of this new 'discipline', I will examine four social considerations to which attention would have to be paid if the discipline were to be introduced into a university. In brief, these are:

1. A theoretical framework rich in potential links with existing frameworks;
2. The creation of 'Chairs' for distinguished defectors from other disciplines;

DIAGRAM 5.1.   Human Communication: The transmission of culture

PUBLIC DIMENSION	*Instrumental*		*Expressive*
Technology	1. Systems or devices to achieve specific social objectives.	↔	2. Social values incorporated in technology.
	↕		↕
Organisations	3. To affect the physical or social environment, e.g. businesses, factories.	↔	4. Embodying beliefs about the physical and social environment, e.g. Churches, political parties.
	↕		↕
Ritual Processes	5. Standardised organisational procedures, often showing no intrinsic link between ends and means, e.g. office parties.	↔	6. Activities with no recognisable economic benefit to the participants, e.g. sport, religious ritual, 'consumption' of mass communications.
	↕		↕
Social Belief Systems	7. Beliefs aimed at social control, e.g. business 'ethos', dogma, doctrine, policy, syllabus.	↔	8. Beliefs which express some insight or ascription of 'value', e.g. 'Science' as a sub-culture, Economics.
	↕		↕
Individual Creations	9. To operate on the physical and social environment, e.g. tools, persuasive documents.	↔	10. To express personal values or idiosyncratic views about the environment, e.g. novels, poems, paintings.
	↕		↕
Personal Beliefs	11. How to survive	↔	12. Why to survive.

PRIVATE DIMENSION

3. Contextual relevance to some identifiable social activity, job, or vocation;
4. Stimulation of similar activity elsewhere—preferably internationally.

The invented discipline may be called 'Human Communication: the transmission of culture'. This title may be more suggestive of what Hirst would call a 'field'; it is perhaps appropriate to an early, slightly 'pre-disciplinary' stage. Perhaps, in its more evolved form, it will acquire some such title as 'Cultural Cybernetics'. Diagram 5.1 shows schematically its basic theoretical features. To show the implications of this 'discipline', the discussion which follows sometimes uses it as an artificial and ironical model of academic structure and procedures, sometimes as a blueprint of what might actually be.

For the sake of argument, culture may be defined here as the reaction to and handling of environment (physical and social) by social groups. Culture may be analysed along four dimensions as follows: an instrumental dimension concerned with the way individuals or groups handle their environment; an expressive dimension concerned with the reaction to environment of individuals or groups; a public dimension concerned with the social processes and techniques used in handling or reacting to environment; a private dimension concerned with individual, often idiosyncratic, ways of handling or reacting to environment which may or may not be subsumed in the public processes. The diagram shows how the relationship between these four dimensions may be described through six categories: technology; organisations; ritual processes; social belief systems; individual creations; and personal beliefs. The important point about the theoretical framework is that all the items which are generated by this matrix of ideas are interrelated. That is to say, personal beliefs are related through individual creations, social belief systems, ritual processes, organisations, to technology and are in turn affected by technology. Each item in the matrix can be interpreted in terms of all the others, and the theoretical framework makes it possible to determine what aspects of culture need to be considered when the transmission of any other aspect of culture is being studied. The contents of any item can, of course, be varied depending on the time or place in which one is interested. Indeed, the 'discipline' may offer contextual relevance for any other existing discipline whose features may be recognised in the scheme. For example, Item 1 deals with engineering.

Engineers are concerned with the building of systems or devices to achieve specific objectives. Inevitably their systems or devices incorporate social values (Item 2) which must be understood if the social meaning of the technique is to be understood. For example, the design of high-speed motor cars implies not only social values concerned with travel, but also a social value concerned with speed. Similarly, disposable cartons for food imply that time is, for one reason or another, more valuable in a given 'culture' than material. Again (Item 3), technological systems require organisations for their manufacture and dissemination. These organisations are instrumental in that they may be specifically designed in the form of factories to make things; but they are nevertheless (Item 4) themselves expressive of certain cultural values. Speed and cheapness of production, for example, may be held to be more important than job satisfaction.

Then, it is clear that organisations are sustained by standard organisational procedures, often having no intrinsic link between means and end. Office parties may be designed to foster good relations among people in a work place—with a view to increasing productivity. Nevertheless, such activities fade into the realm of expressive ritual processes (Item 6) which may have no visible economic benefit to the participants but may express their beliefs about their relations to one another and to a social order at large. The analysis of the ritual processes which sustain organisations will inevitably uncover (Item 7) social belief systems aimed at social control—such as a business ethos. Dogma, doctrine, policy, even a syllabus, are instrumental aspects of social belief systems in that they are designed to control behaviour. Nevertheless, the fact that social groups assent to beliefs implies that analysis should reveal the expressive quality of these belief systems (Item 8). It could, for example, be argued that economics is concerned with the value attached to commodities or ideas by given groups.

But it is obvious that social belief systems, and the ritual processes, organisations, and technology which are the outward and visible sign of the inward and spiritual entity, are not static, are not totally inflexible. Commonly, they are modified by inventions (Item 9), individual creations designed to operate on the physical or social environment. These may take many forms, ranging from physical tools and persuasive documents, to ideas. Whatever instrumental value such individual creations may have, they inevitably (Item 10) express certain personal values or idiosyncratic views about the social or physical environment. Certain types of creation, novels, poems, painting, and other artistic works may have no other object than to express such individual views.

The adoption of a particular system or device of technology reflects culturally certain personal beliefs. Butler made his Erewhonians arrest all technical development at a fixed date, which they estimated to be the point after which such development was likely to be corrupting, and inimical to civilisation. When people cry 'Scrap Concorde', they are expressing a medley of beliefs concerning economic and administrative priorities, health, environment and pollution, and the 'quality of life'. The railway was welcomed both by Tennyson, who saw it as a great metaphor of progress, and by the middle classes, who wanted to transport their sons to public schools. Taking the analysis further, then, one may certainly consider technological phenomena as an aspect of the transmission of culture, relating them in the diagram to Item 11 (how to survive) and Item 12 (why to survive).

This scheme of analysis in the new 'discipline', human communication, could be fruitful in other traditional fields as well. For example, a creative writer—whose novels, poems, plays, etc. would be considered under Item 10—could be regarded, as Malcolm Bradbury (1971) has argued, as a 'central social intelligence'. The interest in analysing a work of creative literature is not only to discover the personal beliefs which it embodies—about how to survive (Item 11) or about why to survive (Item 12)—but also to explore the way it affects and is affected by social belief systems. A rich seam of literary analysis seeks to show how a writer represents or deviates from the social belief system of his culture (Item 7 and Item 8). Perhaps even more interesting is the fact that his individual perceptions undergo various processes of filtration before they reach the public. To make contact with publishing organisations, a writer must go through various 'ritual processes' and must ultimately rely upon organisations (publishing houses) whose directors hold beliefs about their role in the process of transmitting culture and whose organisations, for economic if no other reasons, have a certain mode of operation. Finally (Items 1 and 2), the creative writer's work reaches the public through a technological system—a book, television, radio, etc. It is a matter of intense interest to study the ways in which the shape of technical systems—in turn governed by organisational, ritual and other considerations—affect the shape in which ideas may be expressed. To take two trivial examples: stage lighting has vastly increased the range of effect which the dramatist can command; the use of film in television 'plays' has blurred the category of artistic creation almost beyond recognition.

One more example will show the heuristic fertility of this scheme. At the risk of over-simplification, it may be suggested that science is fundamentally a social belief system expressing the reaction to environment of specific social groups (Item 8). Science considered as a 'sub-culture' may be approached in a variety of ways. Too often it is interpreted only in terms of the technological systems or devices which are the, often accidental, products of the scientific enterprise. At a deeper level, it expresses the life view of the scientist (Item 12) and possibly his personal beliefs about how to survive (Item 11) interpreted in the widest sense. These personal beliefs of individual scientists are commonly translated into ideas for apparatus (Item 9) which control the physical environment in specific ways—but always purposefully, to test the validity of certain theoretical constructions (Item

10) which express views about the environment. Rarely do scientists operate as isolated individuals: most commonly they operate in intellectual 'fields' which may be seen as social belief systems (Item 8) expressing the preoccupations of some social group. Clearly, the way in which the beliefs of the scientific community impinge upon the general public depends on various mediating processes. I have explored these in detail elsewhere (Goodlad, 1973).

(e) *Social requirements for the creation of a new discipline*

This new 'discipline' of Human Communication: the transmission of culture has many potent and fruitful links with other traditional disciplines. Its schematic similarity to certain aspects of sociology, social psychology, and anthropology is a benefit rather than a liability because the ideas and personnel of these other disciplines offer suitable 'territory' for 'intellectual imperialism'. Indeed, this is the first point about the social requirements for the construction of a discipline: it must be recognisable to people brought up in other traditions and it must have a transcending theoretical perspective which permits them to see the 'content' with which they are already familiar in a new—and perhaps more illuminating—light.

The second point is closely related to this. Institutionally, a new discipline is only likely to come into existence by administrative decree from on high. It is in this respect that the overall ethos of the educating institution is of critical importance. The educating institution must accept and nourish the new baby in its midst. A common way of nourishing a new 'discipline' is by the creation of Chairs for distinguished defectors from other disciplines. It is, of course, possible for new disciplines to be laboriously created by self-sacrificing individuals who cut themselves off, often at great personal cost, from the existing structures of other disciplines. Defection is a less drastic and less costly business if bureaucratic recognition of the new discipline is at least in prospect. The history of young disciplines is full of such stories. Morris Ginsberg was the first British Professor of Sociology—coming from philosophy. English Literature as a university discipline at first drew its personnel largely from the classics. Computing Science has a mixed parentage of mathematics and electrical engineering. An important variant of this administrative procedure has been the actual defection, by emigration, of scholars from other countries where the new discipline is already in existence. For example, the social sciences in Britain and in the United States benefited vastly before and during the Second World War by the wholesale emigration of distinguished social scientists from the Continent of Europe.

The third major social requirement for the creation of a new discipline is contextual relevance to some social activity, job, or vocation. This is not to say that a discipline needs to offer a 'training' for a specific job. Manpower goals for education are always a prey to the fickleness of fashion and to the fluctuations of the job market. However, whatever comprehending power and theoretical excellence a new discipline must have, it will require funds. An educating institution may be reluctant to admit another sheep to its fold—but its reluctance is considerably reduced if the sheep has a golden fleece. If the educating institution cannot be persuaded to create Chairs for distinguished defectors, another ploy is as follows. The theoretical comprehensiveness and obvious relevance to a particular occupation or cluster of social problems can be urged upon an outside donor of funds. These funds can then be used to employ 'research assistants' whose terms of contract make them available for teaching low-prestige service courses, ancillary courses, as lateral enrichment to existing disciplines. If these ancillary courses can be adequately grafted on to existing disciplines, the proponents of the new 'discipline' can point to their heavy teaching load and the need for permanent staff to carry it out. With skilful manipulation, it can readily be claimed that new staff become the 'property' of the unit or group teaching the ancillary courses, and the unit or group begins to take on a visible identity. If the cuckoo can sit in the nest long enough, it is likely to find a permanent place in the university establishment.

However, the invented 'discipline' would hardly require any manipulations of such political sophistication for acceptance. Not only is its theoretical structure (as shown in diagram 5.1) one of excellent comprehensiveness; it also has contextual relevance to any occupation whose task is to translate into objects or social action the beliefs of individuals or groups or to interpret the ways in which certain objects or social actions are likely to modify or otherwise constrain these beliefs. While the discipline will not provide 'training' for any specific jobs, the education which it would provide would constitute a suitable background for many occupations—community development, the Church, teaching, broadcasting, etc. The new 'discipline' is, in fact, a house with many mansions where sub-specialisms could flourish within the general theoretical framework.

The fourth social condition for the propagation of a new discipline is the stimulation of similar activity elsewhere—preferably on an international basis. The commonest technique for achieving this is to identify individuals in other disciplines whose interests, or signs of disaffection with their present calling, suggest that they might respond to a new framework for their activities. A conference of such people followed by the publication of a 'reader' or collection of essays and, better still, the foundation of a journal which collects together and ritually defines an area of interest would be a prudent next step. Ultimately, an association or institute should be founded for mutual comfort and international recognition of scholarly excellence wherever it may show itself. Crucially, however, the identification of individuals as belonging to the new 'discipline' and pressure to have them accepted within educating institutions throughout the country, and indeed throughout the world, would ensure a career structure which may be a necessary condition for the growth of a discipline.

From what has been said in this chapter, it should be clear that the mediating influence of the educating institution is critically important in ensuring the survival and subsequent growth of a new discipline. Because disciplines are as much social groupings as intellectual entities, their acceptance or rejection depends as much on the distribution of power within an educating institution as on their relevance or irrelevance to pressing social problems. It is, therefore, important to examine the way in which an educating institution holds together.

It can be seen that, in elaborating this hypothetical situation, I have left large and important areas untouched. For example, I have concentrated almost exclusively on bureaucratic aspects. The procedures for sustaining the discipline have all been interpreted in terms of existing administrative frameworks and with recognition of the need to placate or circumvent 'significant others' whose social power and social prestige determine the concern of educating institutions.

A much more serious exclusiveness has been in the tacit limitation of the realm of a discipline to that of 'objective' knowledge. The authority of this kind of knowledge is, however, repeatedly and vigorously challenged. Even the physical sciences nowadays take into account the fact that the mere act of observation not only determines the framework of interpretation but also modifies, however infinitesimally, the thing observed. In the humanities we might have learnt long ago from Wordsworth, who said 'With the young of both sexes, poetry is, like love, a passion'. But few of these signs have been read in the world of higher education. It is small wonder that recent years have seen outbreaks of fanatical activity in universities from Tokyo to Kent State, from Athens to Essex. The overt motives vary: some are much more clearly political than others. What has been common, and was particularly observable in the sixties, is the emergence of a 'counter culture' whose values are severely at odds with those of the university as traditionally conceived. What are the claims of the new romantics, and to what extent should they be taken into account in the continuing process of redrawing the map of knowledge?

CHAPTER SIX

The New Romantics

This chapter is an example of the very type of intellectual endeavour to which the Counter Culture takes strongest exception. It is verbal, it attempts to deal with passion dispassionately, and it seeks to distance itself from direct experience. It reviews some criticisms of the detached and dispassionate approach to 'objective knowledge' which have emanated from the New Left and other variants of the Counter Culture. It is titled 'The New Romantics' because, although the Counter Culture has taken many forms, there is a common preoccupation with wholeness rather than specialisation, with feeling rather than thought, with synthesis rather than analysis, with consumption rather than production.

It is well-nigh impossible to write anything nowadays about university education without mention of the dramatic upheavals of the 1960s; but I am not here concerned with the causes of the student revolt. Specific and general causes of that revolt, as manifest in different countries, are discussed at length in such books as *Warwick University Limited* edited by E. P. Thompson (1970), *The Student Revolt* by Colin Crouch (1970), *French Revolution 1968* by P. Seale and M. McConville (1968), *University in Revolt: a History of the Columbia Crisis* by J. L. Avorn (1968), *The Campus War* by J. Searle (1972), and *Rebellion in the University* by S. M. Lipset (1972). Colin Crouch, for example (1970, pp. 124–7), has given a classificatory summary of the different sorts of protest. These have included: disruption of meetings to be addressed by unpopular, usually political, speakers; protests concerned with student rights (e.g. free speech); demands for participation in university government; protests at aspects of the relationship between universities and what are considered to be the forces of darkness in the outside world, such as the state (particularly in its defence activities), industry, and racialism; protest stemming from resentment at university disciplinary action; revolts which may have become an end in themselves; and so on. Colin Crouch rightly begins his analysis of the causes of the protests by a chapter 'On Authority'; and it is with the alternative modes of authority embodied in the ideas of the new romantics that I propose to deal.

(a) *The challenge to objective knowledge*

Almost by definition, 'the grey'—i.e. those over thirty—cannot get inside the culture of the young. I must therefore rely largely on the perceptions of such interpreters of the Counter Culture as Theodore Roszak and Charles Reich. Much of the ferment of ideas which they discuss took place in America, but, because my concern is with the qualitative nature of the criticism, its origins in one country or another are of little significance. The challenge to 'objective knowledge' has been made. It is not my purpose to defend or refute any particular position about 'objective knowledge' (such as Popper's 'bucket' or 'searchlight' theories, 1972). I wish, rather, to explore the insights into the question of authority in higher education implied by the critics.

The criticisms are interrelated. However, at the risk of over-simplification, I detach and discuss six. First, there is no such thing as objective knowledge. Second, the life of reason has failed. Third, scientific knowledge, once regarded as the single valid picture of the world, now emerges as one school of consciousness among many. Fourth, Western culture is fanatically verbal. Fifth, the detachment involved in 'objective knowledge' is morally repulsive. Sixth, in education the expressive and the contemplative have been neglected in favour of the instrumental and the exploitative.

The assertion that there is no such thing as objective knowledge derives from the conviction, implicit in the Marxist sociological approach to knowledge, that social structures provide the framework for beliefs, and thus determine what one believes. The New Left, accordingly, emphasises the *class* element in knowledge. The academic interest in the internal consistency of forms of knowledge gives way, for them, to questions about its exogenous characteristics, such as 'whose purpose does knowledge serve?'. A strong stream of Counter Culture criticism urges that experts—and, of course, the education which makes them into experts—are pawns of the military–industrial complex. Syllabuses, therefore, are analysed to show their class bias, the ways in which they support the bourgeois dominance of society. Such course criticism almost always concentrates on making a change in the subject-matter of learning, rather than in the approach to subject-matter.

The second major form of attack on 'objective knowledge' stems from a belief that the life of reason traditionally developed through education has failed. Reich (1972, p. 16) comments on the existence of a universal sense of powerlessness. We seem, he suggests, to be living in a society that no one created and no one wants.

> 'We know what causes crime and social disorder, and what can be done to eliminate those causes. We know the steps that can be taken to create greater economic equality. We are in possession of techniques to fashion and preserve more inhabitable cities and environments. Our problems are vast, but so is our store of techniques; it is simply not being put to use.'

It is not difficult to understand the impatience shown by young idealists with much that goes on in universities. The writing of an elegant monograph on the use of the subjunctive in Norman French must seem to be fiddling while Rome burns. Not surprisingly, then, one reaction to the frustrations in the life of the mind is to turn one's back upon it. The proliferation of sects and meditation groups, of fundamentalist or irrationalist sub-cultures among undergraduates dramatises this rejection. Indeed, the emergence of interest in myth, religion and ritual as a countering of rationality is an important phenomenon in itself. It leads Roszak (1971, p. 146) to observe that:

> 'It is quite impossible any longer to ignore the fact that our conception of intellect has been narrowed disastrously by the assumption, especially in the academies, that the life of the spirit is: (1) a lunatic fringe best left to artists and visionaries; (2) a historical boneyard for antiquarian scholarship; (3) a highly specialised adjunct of professional anthropology; (4) an antiquated vocabulary still used by the clergy, but intelligently soft-pedalled by its more enlightened members. Along none of these approaches can the living power of myth, ritual, rite be expected to penetrate the intellectual establishment and have any existential (as opposed to merely academic) significance. If conventional scholarship does touch these areas of human experience, it is ordinarily with the intention of compiling knowledge, not with the hope of salvaging value.'

In fact, the angry denials of the Counter Culture have redirected attention in a very positive way to forms of knowledge too easily neglected in Western culture.

The third criticism, which demotes scientific knowledge to the status of one form of consciousness among many, takes exception to the fact that it remains a school of consciousness to which other modes of consciousness defer. Again, Roszak (1972, p. 34) is the clearest exponent:

'Scientific knowing becomes, within the artificial environment, the orthodox mode of knowing; all else defers to it. Soon enough the style of mind that began with the natural scientists is taken up by imitators throughout the culture. Until we find ourselves surrounded by every manner of scientific–technical expert, all of them purporting to know as the scientists know: dispassionately, articulately, on the basis of empirical evidence or experiment, without idiosyncratic distortion, and if possible by the intervention of mathematics, statistics, or a suitably esoteric methodology.'

Roszak's contention is that, as a culture, we are obsessed with the hard-edged focus of the scientist's impersonal eye, at the expense of the sort of peripheral vision which we regard as imprecise. In this way, he says, we become ever more learnedly stupid: 'Our experience dissolves into a congeries of isolated puzzles, losing its overall grandeur'.

This criticism leads on compellingly to the fourth—that is, that Western culture is fanatically verbal. Here there is a gap of crucial importance between the teachers and the taught, and the same thing can appear quite differently to those on either side of the chasm. Reich, for instance, has at one point (pp. 132–4) a lyrical evocation of the aspects of human experience we have lost. These include magic and mystery, awe, awareness of death, spontaneity, play, reflection, wholeness, expanded consciousness, new values. But these are things which many university teachers would claim to find in their subjects. Poetry and mathematics alike are not only formal modes of organising experience; they are also ways of generating new experience. Universities, perceived by the Counter Culture as a shield *against* experience, may represent for faculty members the richest source of experience which Western culture has to offer. But verbal transformation—which can and should be the very means by which experience is shared—becomes, when used in universities as an analytical technique, a means of distancing. The attack on the verbal nature of Western culture, and thus of much higher education, indicates the pressing need to re-emphasise the experiential quality of learning. If the physics professor cannot communicate his experience of the passion and the delicacy of physics, he has failed as a teacher. If he has not himself felt the passion and the delicacy, he has no business to be there at all.

The fifth criticism follows logically, for it is a condemnation of the detachment necessarily associated with 'objective knowledge'. The conventional academic approach is felt to deny the important principle of personal commitment, and its coolness is repellent. Sophisticated education, Roszak complains, teaches appreciative gestures but avoids the white-hot experience of authentic vision.

A delusive belief in objectivity, the over-valuing of rationality, scientific knowledge, verbalism and detachment—criticisms of all these culminate in the accusation that contemplation has been neglected in favour of an exploitative approach to knowledge. The Counter Culture stressed the expressive quality of knowledge rather than its instrumental value. In this rediscovery of the emotional satisfaction, the aesthetic pleasure of understanding for its own sake, may lie the most important single legacy of the Counter Culture. The perception itself existed before the revolts in higher education, and is expressed in, for example, *Personal Knowledge* (1958) by Michael Polanyi. What the Counter Culture may have done is to help to make Polanyi's kind of perception public. It is both significant and touchingly ironical that an assertion of the contemplative virtues should have been associated with the excesses of the student revolution.

(b) *The claims of subjectivity*

The causes of these student protests are of less interest here than the behaviour and ideas associated with them. Even academics whose institutions have not suffered major disruption may have been puzzled by the apparently able student who drops out—and, having done so, chooses a life of apparently aimless drifting. Higher education is surprised and hurt by its drop-outs, but, because they are 'no trouble', it is not provoked into action or fundamental re-thinking. The political exponents of the Counter Culture are often only too visible—perhaps sitting in the administration building. The drop-out, because he is not visible, may not be experienced in the university as a challenge to authority. But he is.

The first type of attack on 'objective knowledge' expresses a preoccupation with questions about life's purpose, subordinating 'How shall we know?' to the existentially more vital 'How shall we live?' A preoccuption with different sorts of consciousness is the very hallmark of the Counter Culture. The revolutionary version of the Counter Culture urges that the university is but one institution of a repressive industrial culture which must be overthrown in the early stages of the Revolution. But the less politicised, more gentle, version of the emphasis on consciousness—the *'consciousness* consciousness' of which Roszak (1971, p. 62) writes—has a positive value in redirecting attention to questions of life's purpose.

If careful provision for such matters is made in the university curriculum, students as a whole have not noticed it. A common term of criticism is 'irrelevant', a word which carries strong though rather confused connotations both of dissociation from their own absorbing and important personal lives and of ineffectiveness in dealing with manifestly urgent social problems. The apparent impotence of universities in this respect is thrown into greater relief, and is the more disillusioning, when they are seen to be heavily committed not only to the education of technical experts but also—through their research programmes—to industrial and governmental interests in science and technology. Robert Nisbet (1971) attributes much of the disillusionment of the young in universities to 'the degradation of the academic dogma'. This degradation, he says, is consequent upon the wholesale importation into universities of centres, bureaux, institutes, etc., the effect of which has been to draw the energies of their faculty away from teaching to research. Like many other commentators, Nisbet regards as misguided the policy of trying to make universities meet national needs directly. Traditionally, he says, universities provide an *indirect* form of service. They have not been, are not, and probably should not be organised to take direct action in society. This recalls Moberly's observation (1949, p. 39) that a university is a 'thought-organisation', not a 'will-organisation', and that its aim is understanding rather than action: 'It is a society for the pursuit of knowledge and not for the promotion of this cause or the prevention of that abuse.'

Academic detachment is difficult enough in any case to justify to intelligent young reformers eager for action. The difficulty is immeasurably increased when they see the important social, political and economic spin-offs of university activities. If the neutrality of the university is compromised anyway, they argue, why not leave off calculating the number of micro-curies which may dance on a pin-head and get busy in the world of work?

The elders can, of course, reply that the whole matter is more complex than students are prepared to think. An important point about neutrality, for instance, which is often overlooked has been well stated by John Searle (1972, p. 183):

'The traditional theory of university neutrality is not that the university avoids having any social consequences but that it is open to the expression of all points of view and it does not take institutional stands on controversial social and political questions (except in so far as its educational mission requires it to do so . . .). One might say that the implicit theory of neutrality is not a neutrality of *effects* (consequences, results) but a neutrality of *institutional intent.*'

But this too raises as many questions as it answers. *When*, the student may reasonably ask, does its educational mission require it to take an institutional stand? The student protest in this field has been valuable in focusing attention on the need, first, to define types of work appropriate to a university, and to make clear to undergraduates what these are; secondly, to recognise and understand the limits of rationality.

The political form of 'Consciousness III', as Charles Reich calls it, then judges universities to be, at best, irrelevant, and ineffectual. The quieter form, *'consciousness* consciouness', is no better satisfied. Roszak writes (1971, p. 208) of 'the myth of objective consciousness', against which he advances two objections. First, discovery is the principle of ordering in science: but the order comes from the scientist's mind, and this observation in itself should make one suspicious of the objectivity claimed. Second—and more important—the very process of ordering experience is destructive, for it implies that the experience *itself* has no validity. The specialised selectivity of science, which has led to the emergence of experts on even the most intimately personal regions of human life, is particularly dangerous because it devalues the experience of ordinary people.

To challenge the authority of the objective (even if objectivity is not an illusion) is to exalt the authority of the subjective. This has an important bearing on the relationship of the generations, for it reduces or destroys the status-authority of the elders.

Part of the authority of the elders, as the Counter Culture sees it, resides in what Reich has called Consciousness II, which believes in *control*—believes, that is, that society will function best if it is planned, organised, rationalised, administered. In contrast, the consciousness of the New Romantics, Consciousness III, believes in openness to all experience, without the mediation of intellect or control. A large part of its endeavour is concerned with trying to escape imposed consciousness. It is therefore deeply suspicious of logic, of rationality, of analysis, and of principles (p. 216). This is why the use of drugs has been a distinguishing feature of the Counter Culture. Consciousness is enlarged, experience is generated without control. Marijuana throws emphasis on 'now-ness' as reality, taking people outside the enclosed system, and releasing them from the domination of their thought. It makes *unreal* what society takes most seriously: time, schedules, rational connections, competition, anger, excellence, authority, private property, law, status, the primacy of the state, the standards imposed by other people and society. Accepted patterns of thought must be broken: therefore, 'rational' thought must be opposed by 'non-rational' thought—drug-thought, mysticism, impulses (p. 301).

Openness entails an absence of reserve, a totality of commitment which has a message for higher education. It becomes important not only to emphasise the intrinsic values of *content* but also to highlight the forms of commitment implicit in the way in which content is approached. Although mastery is a useful stage in an academic discipline, it is neither the starting-point nor the finishing-point. The true starting-point is *attachment*. The true end-product is a relationship to some area of knowledge which, having been mastered, leads to enjoyment; which, therefore, is a living relationship.(28)

The bureaucratic nature of the university, and the decreasing possibility of intimate personal contact beween teacher and taught, have led to neglect of the existential quality of university work. The desire for knowledge is a sort of fever—more caught than taught. Similarly, the quality of commitment in students' attachment to their subjects of study must somehow be given a chance to communicate itself. University teachers could be, for example, much more sensitive to the reasons which lead students to choose their subjects : sensitive not as benevolent onlookers, but as professional and professing teachers whose job it is to know both the nature of their task and the skills of their art. Would an engineer build a bridge, however great his competence in drawing plans, without a close acquaintance with both the properties of his materials and the features of the terrain? Among the university population are the literature student who writes poetry and produces plays; the geographer who wanders the world with sleeping bag; the electrical engineering student who ran the school projector and 'did' the lights for the school play; the mechanical engineer who spends more time stripping and rebuilding his old car than riding in it; the history student who spends his vacations hacking his way through the undergrowth following the track of a disused canal; the social science student who wishes to be involved in social interaction, not just to study it. There are, of course, geography departments in which lecturers and students together pack their sleeping bags and set off for the Ruwenzori mountains or the tin mines of Cornwall; student drama which is an absorbing way of life, while the drama professor is the very antithesis of reverent *signior*. But, what matters is not the presence or absence of 'project' activities or the degree of mateyness between teacher and student. Commitment needs to be both felt and shared from both sides. The careful interweaving of detachment with involvement may be a necessary condition of success in higher education.

(c) *Personal commitment and the question of goals*

Personal commitment involves the question of goals. The attempt of the Counter Culture to define new goals for living is one of its most dramatic features. Reich (1972, p. 202) has noted how Consciousness III feels that the goals of Consciousness II (status, security, possessions, respect, etc.) are not merely wrong, they are *unreal*. Consciousness III, he urges (p. 293) seeks to restore the non-material elements of man's existence to their proper pre-eminence as goals, and to put science and technology in their proper place as tools of man rather than as determinants of his existence. The challenge, like other challenges of the Counter Culture, deserves respect. Is the Gross National Product a proper goal for living?

If, in the view of the Counter Culture, technology and the discoveries of science are justified only in the service of man, the corollary is that the natural world does not exist merely for his plundering. Perhaps the present generation is the first which has been able to afford itself the luxury of taking the long-term leisured view of means and ends. The exploitative approach to nature diminishes in importance and justification. Conservation, preservation, a concern with wholeness are now possible. With such fertile ground, it should not be too difficult to re-establish the value of learning as understanding rather than as access to exploitation. This may have some relevance to the 'manpower' goal discussed in Chapter 2. For it seems less and less likely that supply and demand will ever be perfectly matched, or that the highly trained graduate can be sure of getting the exact type of work for which he has seemed to be so minutely preparing himself. The need will still be for a large supply of experts, but even more for educated people of wisdom and adaptability. In this context a more restful, less anxious and competitive philosophy becomes highly desirable.

Against this background of thought and feeling, the students' call for 'relevance' comes to mean more than manifest preparation for a job, and more even than a relationship to the events and causes of the day. Students may not quite know what they are asking for: the insistent demand that wells up from within is no less serious and significant. Academics are not always sure what—except in superficial terms of a prescribed syllabus—they are teaching, or why. If the Counter Culture has stimulated teachers to examine the philosophical and social significance of what they teach, and to recapture the passion and the singlemindedness of their own commitment to learning, it will have done a necessary work.

CHAPTER SEVEN

The Plural Thrust

If universities are creative centres of plural culture, what is the nature of their commitment? How does one recognise a school of English and a school of Chemistry to be legitimately part of the same institution? How does one decide what subjects are to be admitted? And, in broad terms, what styles of teaching are appropriate in the university's approach to knowledge?

In Chapter 6 I have argued that relevance is intelligible only in a context of commitment, that engagement in an intellectual discipline begins with an act of personal attachment; in short, that innocence about the emotional load of a form of study is no longer tolerable. It does not, however, follow that because totally objective knowledge is neither attainable nor desirable the only criterion for the admission of the subject to the body of university studies is anybody's whim—or, if not anybody's, a sufficiently vocal somebody's. The institutional neutrality of the university is a positive, not negative, form of neutrality. Although pluralism cannot logically justify its own or any other approach to knowledge, the mode of study implied by pluralism is an important and valuable one, central to the intellectual life of the university and, therefore, central to any identification of the authority which the university may hope to exercise in society at large.

In a plural society, where no statement of belief in 'ultimate' truth commands assent, there can be no permanent institutions reflecting cosmic order. There is a great need, however, for one type of institution with persistently recognisable shape from which change can be measured, and which permits and encourages the unending review of hypotheses which pluralism implies. Indeed, certain facets of university life which dramatise the idea of such an institution remain in the memories of former students who have, perhaps intuitively, grasped the value of contexts which permit the refinement of categories of interpretation—the seminar room with chalk-scrawled black-board, the study bedroom filled at three in the morning with waving arms and empty coffee cups, the urgent 'If . . . then . . .' of the draft paper, etc. The university does not, of course, have a pre-rogative of such phenomena,. There is often very little difference be-tween an industrial research laboratory and a university research laboratory. Again, the critical permissiveness of the university semi-nar may appear in any social context. The point is that the university makes such activity its business.

(a) *What makes a subject suitable for university study?*

This 'seminar' mode of realising the positive thrust of pluralism in turn suggests criteria by which a subject may be recognised as suitable for incorporation in the work of the university. Universities have always been vocational—with theology, followed by medicine, law, and later engineering, among others, as central disciplines. Why not, then, it is sometimes asked, admit cookery? In fact, cookery *has* been admitted—but as the study of nutrition and dietetics, the theoretical counterparts of the intensely practical and culturally important pri-mary activity. The main criterion for including a subject in the work of a university is that the subject requires a considerable body of theoretical knowledge. Although in most cases such theoretical know-ledge underpins and indeed generates practical activity, it is always centrally of interest because of the uncertainties to which it points. Indeed, one might even go on to assert that unless a subject of study involves uncertainties, it is just not suitable for incorporation in the university.

The crucial task, then, of the university is to stimulate theoretical enquiry involving uncertainty, and to provide the institutional con-text in which uncertainty can be tolerated. In a situation where the only thing certain is that everything is uncertain, consensus about practically every social, political, religious, or other issue will be lacking. However, one form of consensus is the necessary condition for the process of enquiry to take place at all : consensus that intel-lectual conflict should be separated from personal or social conflict. The central role of the educating institution is to create an atmosphere in which intellectual conflict can be maintained without too much personal or psychic violence. The fact that practice so often fails to correspond with theory in no way invalidates the concept.

Conflict may be implicit in any area of knowledge. The positive thrust of pluralism, institutionally embodied in the university, is to make possible the creative use of conflicting intellectual positions. If, for example, one questions the pharmaceutical approach to medicine, one may find that it is cheaper and more effective in terms of the numbers of people benefiting to institute a lot of weight-watching clubs than to spend the same amount of money on intensive research into new drugs. It might, in fact, be better to study health rather than medicine. Even within the university, any such radical suggestion as this threatens so many vested interests that, but for an institutionalised framework of speculation, it might never be possible to carry investigations forward. Because challenge to one's temporary intellectual certainties is painful, and is usually taken personally (for academics are no less human than other men), deliberate exposure of one's ideas to judgment from the standpoint of another discipline requires an act of courage. But this is what pluralism requires.

Such is the power of paradigms and the social solidarity of disciplinary groupings that even the hard sciences can slide into the position of seeming to teach certainties rather than to teach uncertainties —to make it appear to students that experimental procedures are designed to 'prove the facts' rather than being a systematic effort to 'disprove'. Lateral enrichment of a scientific or engineering degree with courses from the humanities may be tolerated only if the enriching subjects do not challenge in any fundamental way the apparent certainties of the host discipline. Yet, the real value of non-technical studies for, say, engineers is to generate that feeling of the uncertainty, of the temporary and hypothetical status of *all* knowledge, which is central to the university approach.

The deliberate quest for theoretically significant uncertainty thrusts emphasis inevitably onto procedure. In the sciences this takes the form of research techniques; in the humanities of scholarship. Where techniques are themselves the subject of theoretical uncertainty, one can soon feel as lost as in a hall of mirrors. For example, it was inevitable that sooner or later sociology would become interested in itself, and seem thereby to sow the seeds of its own destruction. A narcissistic process of self-evaluation could be set afoot by each new sociology of sociology (see, for example, R. W. Friedrichs, 1970), which must surely lead on to a sociology of sociologies of sociology, and so on and so on. However, the determination exhibited by such writing to keep in review the nature of the discipline's commitment can only be applauded. If a discipline in a university becomes too much beholden to a sectional interest of the world outside the university, there is a danger that its essential quality of disinterested enquiry become lost to sight.

Because this concept of disinterestedness is central in the university's attitude to knowledge, no apology is needed for investigating it further.

(b) *The meaning of disinterestedness*
A discipline has vitality when it has contextual relevance to some occupation or occupations. Similarly, an institution is really alive only when it has its feet in the ground of social need. A distinction should not be drawn between 'interest' and 'disinterestedness', in which the latter is interpreted as 'being uninterested about serving society'.

There is a continuum of expanding interest as one moves from interests which can be too narrow and too much just servicing, towards wider and wider concepts of content of subjects. Even the most remote academic subject ultimately has to have its roots in society and the needs of society, though this becomes less and less obvious to the more 'limited' people practising the discipline. Institutions of higher education carry servicing the interests of society along with those of wider range.(28)

Being disinterested does not exclude what is practical. Engineering studies, for example, can be disinterested—provided that they are pursued with a backing of theory, and not simply the theory needed to do a specific job.(26) The word 'disinterested' suggests a wider range of interests, either directly involved or playing on the subject. 'Disinterested' studies are not useless ones, but studies conceived in the widest possible context.

To state in this way an ideal of disinterested study is not to suggest that it is easy of achievement. When they come to university, students have rarely experienced disinterestedness in the sense outlined—having been devoted to getting through their examinations. And indeed, the social pressure on universities for degree certificates can only too easily corrupt university study in like manner. Again, pressures of the academic market-place may force staff into a felicific calculus where not to publish is to perish, or where insufficient busyness may deprive a research group of a continuation grant from sponsoring foundation or research council. So delicate is the balance between love and prostitution in intellectual matters, that academic freedom is a subject of endless fascination in universities.

People are often suspicious of the 'applied', not because they are obsessed with the purity of studies but because they have strong views on value-questions. University students are often suspicious of Business Schools because they may support a system the students do not approve. A suspicion of the 'applied' can exist even among those who are least 'pure'.(31) But to show that the impetus for a particular study is bureaucratic, inspired by considerations external to the university, is not to show that the studies themselves are biased. Rather it may be presumed that universities are invited to carry out studies for government because universities are expected to bring to bear on the subject the widest possible range of considerations, and not to be constrained by considerations of political expediency. Certainly, however, in any study, one would like to see a clear statement of the interests involved, particularly if these seem to come other than from the immediate theoretical preoccupations of the discipline.

Can disinterestedness and commitment, then, be reconciled? At one level, yes. Operationally, a commitment to detachment is perhaps the principle common to all university work. One's concern, however, is properly with the highest level of individuality. It needs no pleading that higher education, university education especially, must do more than produce experts in specialisms from surgery to history, from economics to archaeology. How, then, without losing the essence of its intellectual character, can higher education stimulate qualities such as tolerance, aesthetic perception, sympathy, and personal commitment?

(c) *The reconciliation of disinterestedness and commitment*

Disinterestedness demands that personal feelings shall not impede knowledge or judgment; it is, therefore, necessary to be explicit about the widest possible range of considerations applicable to a subject. But explicitness may destroy important intuitions—one does not perceive the beauty of a rose by counting its petals. If, as Colin Crouch suggests, in the revolutionary concept of the university everything is political, by contrast problems in the conventional university are likely rather to be seen as subjects for analysis, and there is a tendency to concentrate exclusively on points of detail. How, then, is a student to use the approved techniques and yet remain both individual and committed?

Perhaps both the individuality and the commitment reside in the motivation. The purposes of individuals, their motivations for study, are of course extrinsic to the subject-matter of their study. Geology, for example, may appeal to the dreamer interested in the history of the physical world or it may appeal to the speculator interested to know where oil may be found. It is often, perhaps usually, the commitment to a vocation which gives a person's study its impetus. Indeed, commitment is both the starting point and the finishing point in most people's experience of university education. The choice of a field of study expresses commitment to certain ideas, and probably to a specific profession. Similarly, the graduate must ultimately have some conception of the social relevance and social purpose of his study.

The problem is not a new one: it has, for example, been present in the discipline of theology for many years. Theology will always remain suspect by other disciplines because it raises questions of truth in odd and complex ways, requiring as it does a compatibility between the demands of reason and the determination to remain fruitfully responsive to what it chooses to regard as the 'coercive' element in reality. This complexity derives from the history and variety of activities which comprise a religion—its doctrines, its acts within history (and therefore its life as a social polity or confession), but also its scriptures, its worship and its liturgy. This has to be harmonised, explained, and brought into equilibrium anew in each generation.

This is the interpretative role of theology—internal to the needs of the believing community, but not self-enclosed.(5)

Indeed, the theologian's external (as distinct from internal) usefulness consists in his ability to deal *adequately* and in a general way with the complex phenomena of commitment (or assent). It is a field the theologian shares with philosophers and sociologists, but especially with poets and novelists. He needs therefore to recognise not merely the overlap but the boundaries and distinctions. He begins with the imagination, as he responds to the mysteries and ambiguities of scriptural language. He reflects. He analyses his motives, clarifies and generalises his conclusions. The knowledge he acquires, however, remains too highly ambiguous. It finds its completion in action. But, for the believer, such completion is social: religious explanation and act cohere within a community of acts. All forms of commitment or assent have one factor in common: the extent to which they raise questions of truth within a complex structure which belongs essentially to and is inseparable from the means of verification. It cannot be by-passed or reduced to simpler form without a complete change of character.

Theology must be taught on the assumption that of all acts of commitment or assent, religion appears to be the most highly complex: and the theologian needs to be taught how to detect whether the character claimed for a religious assent is adequately complex, or whether (on the other hand) it could be simpler: it is just as dangerous to believe too much as to believe too little. It is perhaps when theologians fall off this tight-rope that they give the impression that theological understanding can take place without religious commitment. The theologian's task is to distinguish between (and yet reconcile) the initial wholeness of the response of faith and its articulations subsequently into theological notions and concepts. This is a major form of that distinction (and reconciliation) between feeling and thought.

Although the distinction and reconciliation between feeling and thought is, perhaps, at its most dramatic in theology, it is present in many other disciplines too. The insistence of the Counter Culture on personal commitment and personal involvement is only an extreme statement of what many students feel. Having come to university from a world of action and hoping to return to such a world, many of them may be unable to tolerate protracted spells of 'disinterested' study. If the personal commitment which leads a student into a form of study fades, that is to say if his sense of purpose weakens, he may cease to study altogether. If the university believes it to be no part of its business to imbue a student with a sense of purpose, there remains the problem of where that sense of purpose is to come from. A plural society positively requires people who have been taught to conduct enquiries under the control and for the sake of their beliefs. Perhaps what is required is the deliberate provision for periods of reflection within a degree course and within each subject taught within a degree course.(5)

(d) *Modes of study appropriate for realising the positive thrust of pluralism*

On the large scale, what is probably required is an extension of the 'sandwich' principle of education for many students. At present the most common model for this is in undergraduate training for industry. A big firm such as ICI or Shell sponsors the student over, say, a five-year contract, giving him work-experience in the factory or engineering plant in the first year, covering fees and subsistence in university or polytechnic for the next three, and taking him back for a final year of training 'on the job'. There are variants. Sometimes a year of work-experience comes in the middle of the university course. There is, also, within several university disciplines themselves, a practical or 'field' element. Medical students spend increasing periods of their long course in hospitals, and experiments are now being made in giving them some hospital experience at a much earlier stage than formerly. Foreign-language students usually 'sandwich' between their second and final years a year of teaching or comparable experience in the country of the language they are studying. Expeditions and work at field centres are, of course, normal practice for biologists and geographers, while mining, agricultural or engineering students are encouraged to take vacation work connected with the practical skills of their study. Outside the university, periods of teaching are an essential part of the course in colleges of education, while for art, drama and music students—and, of course, theological students—the commitment to practical professional work is a very important element of their studies.

A college of education course as at present constituted is a sandwich of a different kind—a three-decker sandwich, too! Periods of observation and teaching in schools alternate with subject study and theoretical aspects of education. This has all the elements necessary for highly motivated study and an excellent integration of theory and practice. Unfortunately, it does not always turn out like that. Some students, no more eager than their university or polytechnic counterparts to see their institution as an educating institution, envisage their courses from the outset as like a typing course, only more elaborate—a training in techniques, to be mastered as slickly and rapidly as possible. Others, university students *manqués*, are chiefly interested in their academic studies—the less utilitarian and the less obviously applicable the better. Too often there is little synthesis within the learner's mind of the different parts of the course. A mixture does not spontaneously become a compound. A clear understanding of the intricacies of 'transfer', and deliberate and skilful procedures to ensure it, are necessary if the blend of theory and practice, of 'interested' and 'disinterested', is to become a synthesis. Yet within the college field the successes, when they are found, are so impressive that they may be taken as models in discussion of the sandwich principle in university studies. That version consists in a deliberately planned and unified alternation of 'committed' and 'disinterested' work.

In some colleges and departments of education, attempts are being made to work out a new principle. The period of practice becomes the focal point or spearhead of a complex programme of highly theoretical work. Though the 'skill' element of the practice must not be ignored, the object of the whole undertaking is not to achieve a readily recognisable proficiency: emphasis is thrown much less on the visible product, much more on the process. Something like one day a week (the timing arrangements in the university are slightly different) is set aside for group analysis of the students' *accounts* of their experiences, and for mutual learning and reference to authorities in psychology, philosophy, history and so on. Supervision is less, consultation more frequent. In supervision, the judicial element becomes smaller, the descriptive and creative larger. In the group analyses, reported successes or failures acquire a different significance, since they are equally good material for joint learning. Some colleges succeed, despite the organisational difficulties, in incorporating the school teachers in these analytical sessions, and some have even arranged to hold, at the same time as the students are practising in school, theoretical analyses by the teachers of the schemes covered by the students.

It needs no demonstration that students are 'interested' in their teaching practice. If, indeed, they cannot make that total response so urgently advocated by the Counter Culture, it is part of the tutor's task to set them free to be able to do so. In the theoretical group sessions the prevailing tone is that of disinterestedness. Personal emotions, often intense, associated with the teaching experience, are distanced, objectified, made tolerable in the process of analysis, appraisal and the appeal to authority. But the process is no simple matter of lumping together everything labelled 'commitment' and putting it on one side, and everything labelled 'detachment' on the other. The alternation is much more like that of an alternating current. In the teaching situation there must be pauses for objective appraisal, particularly self-appraisal. The supervising tutor, whose general function is to support and release, must also sometimes help the student to achieve 'distancing' in a review of the lesson. Correspondingly, during the group sessions a new kind of personal commitment, inherent in the mutual relationships, will certainly develop and become a very important educative experience.

Can something like this be achieved in many university disciplines? Probably it could if periods of total personal involvement or commitment to practical activity could alternate with periods of 'disinterested', critical, yet permissive, reflection within the context of the university seminar. I mention the seminar advisedly. (The word 'permissive', too, is deliberate.) Not all forms of university teaching encourage reflection and criticism. If emphasis is to be thrust on uncertainty, teaching styles must be evolved which encourage and expose legitimate uncertainty. But this does not mean the uncertainty born of sheer ignorance; one must know a good deal in order to know what still requires to be known! It should also be added that commitment does not invariably presuppose practical work. Not all studies have a manifestly practical component. The most committed and intensely personal activity of a literary student may be the writing of poetry or fiction—not a practical activity in the ordinary sense of the term. It may also be that in some subjects the most disinterested part is the practical; the most committed, the seminar. One can envisage a physics student being severely objective in his work with an oscilloscope (committed only in his dedication to accuracy), but being personally and passionately committed in a seminar discussion on Strontium 90.

If the study of value-questions in a plural society is not to be completely neutered—if disinterestedness is not to become uninterestedness—a teaching style is required which will engage students in the study of value-questions, but which will not involve any form of coercion or pressure by the teacher for students to adopt the moral position to which *he* is committed. An example of such a style is available in Gerald Collier's account of some experiments in moral education for student teachers.

Collier opened his course with the showing of a film, *Twelve Angry Men*, a study of a jury at a murder trial. The jury's tentative verdict is 'guilty'; however, a single member pleads some discussion of the evidence and begins to sow doubts which eventually lead to a reversal of this verdict. The film is a study of an individual of more than usual integrity who is able to maintain his uneasy doubts in the face of opposition and indifference. At the close of the film, the class was divided into small groups ('syndicates') of five persons. The syndicates were then issued with assignments, consisting of several questions on the mode of influence of the man of integrity and a final question asking for a definition of 'integrity' on the basis of this film. Each syndicate was required to hand in a report on the questions posed. The lecturer assembled these reports in a formal lecture of twenty to thirty minutes accompanied by a duplicated summary, and a plenary discussion was held. A similar procedure was used with other films and with books which the students were asked to read.

These assignments had several objects. The first was to study a group of figures of exceptional integrity, attempting to get inside their minds, to observe the pressures at work on them, to follow the interaction between them and their associates, and to understand the nature of their influence on other people. The second object was to provide an opportunity for the students to argue out the validity or otherwise of the judgments and decisions made by the characters studied, in film or in print, testing their own judgment in specific and complex situations against that of the figures studied and against that of their fellows in the syndicate and the class. Collier suggested that the moral judgments of young people are often based on black-and-white principles, on an over-simple interpretation of complex situations, and such syndicate exercises can develop a richer appreciation of balancing factors and claims.

The third object was to define the moral quality of 'integrity'—one of the virtues most consistently advocated and held up as an ideal by the Western tradition—in order to see more clearly what this quality is and what it is not, thus giving the student some experience of the conceptual clarification needed in any fully developed moral thinking. The fourth object was to clarify the nature of the arguments involved in reaching the moral judgments studied—the kind of evidence selected and inferences drawn, the assimilation of concrete situations to different value-principles, the deciding on the relevance of particular principles or the priorities among them.

The intellectual processes to which students were exposed are less important, in the context of the present chapter, than the methods by which the study was organised. Collier commented on the method of organisation of the students' working situation as follows. The central core of the course was the work done within the syndicates, and the essence of this was the attempts, through argument within the syndicate, to ascertain what views they wished to report in answer to the questions posed in the assignments. The material of the discussions held within the syndicates came either from the films seen or from the texts read. When the tutor summarised the syndicate reports in his lecture, he revealed as much of his own views as appeared relevant.

Collier claimed that this type of organisation has an important bearing on several aspects of moral education. In the first place, the students are in general unable to learn the tutor's views on the questions raised until after their own views have been formulated. They are therefore less likely to be influenced either towards or against conformity. Secondly, the lack of mutual understanding and confidence between the generations can easily, in normal seminar contexts, be masked by habits of politeness and the pressures of examinations, whereas the syndicates are able to formulate their views before the tutor selects them for his lecture-summary. It is true that the tutor may still misread the evidence of the reports: nevertheless, the evidence of students' thinking is likely to be available in more decisive form than in an orthodox seminar discussion. The structure gives the opportunity for the students to move a debate in fresh directions, to explore new approaches to value-questions.

It may be argued that the tutor *ought* to be influencing the students' moral judgment, since he is (or should be) wiser and more sophisticated in his views. It may also be objected that a tutor cannot *help* influencing the moral views of students—and that such influence is inappropriate in a plural society. Collier suggested that the tutor's appropriate mode of influence is through the provision of assignments felt by students to be relevant to their interests and experience, the bringing of significant texts to their attention in a setting which enables them to make effective use of them, the pressing of certain questions of the kind already outlined, the creation of a climate of genuine enquiry in ethical questions, and the treatment of their views in a way which demonstrates that he respects and values them.

Thirdly, in moral questions especially, the personal factors loom large. Students who have decided the membership of their own syndicates are likely to be better able to tolerate the inevitable divergencies of response and orientation which have to be worked through. An important part of a student's moral education lies in learning to accept and appreciate the unexpected depth or shallowness of his own responses as well as the richness and the diverse contributions of other people's. Each syndicate tends to develop its own culture, in which mutual understanding and insights are important factors, and individuals are caught up in the more intimate and detailed searching into one another's outlook.

Finally, the intense and protracted debates *under the above conditions* appear to help students to clarify their judgments and improve their analytical skill. One can observe them developing their powers of deliberation and exploration in dealing with complex issues and strengthening their capacity for joint thinking and judgment. They learn a good deal about themselves, making explicit their own inner, unverbalised responses and discovering in some degree where their own deeper priorities lie. On the cognitive side they learn above all to interrelate more effectively abstractions of academic sources with the particularities of personal experience and response. Collier acknowledged that in these particular courses the least successful part, perhaps, had been the training in the analysis of moral argument and inference; the questions in the assignments had evidently offered insufficient scope in this direction. (See also Collier, 1969.)

The syndicate method thus described has features which should prove attractive in any disciplines where questions of personal belief and moral commitment are involved. In universities, where the ideal of disinterested enquiry is respected, and where institutionalised scepticism is the appropriate realisation of intellectual pluralism, there is a danger that subjects generating strong emotions or involving deeply held passions will be ignored. Again, as pressures on universities to educate increasingly large numbers of students increase, there is a danger that emphasis will move onto instruction based on mass-lectures and formal assignments, to the neglect of teaching structures which permit and encourage mutuality. Intellectual reflection, aided by the formal processes of research or scholarship, needs to be balanced by activity which is positively valuative. The problem is to know how this should be done.

Where teaching style has to be limited to classroom exercises, the syndicate method combines moral engagement with more highly structured reflection within the theoretical perspective offered by a discipline. But opportunities for an engagement–reflection pattern of work are immeasurably increased if students can be given the chance to deepen their sense of social commitment by carrying out direct practical service to the community within the context of the curriculum. *Education and Social Action* (Goodlad, 1975) gives examples of how this can be achieved in such subjects as law, engineering, town planning, theology, sociology, and modern languages. To combine community service with the curriculum in higher education may seem to negate the very possibility of detachment, of disinterested study. And indeed it might do so if the political, religious, or other moral motivation which generates social concern were allowed to obliterate the peculiarly academic elements of study, the disinterestedness which exposes an idea to the widest possible range of viewpoints. But, by a judicious mix of projects, summer schemes, sandwich arrangements, and so on, action and reflection can be combined.

Modes of study have been emphasised in this chapter because they must contain the tensions which inevitably exist between feeling and thought, and between commitment and detachment. 'Interests' of one kind and another generate the goals of higher education; disinterestedness characterises its methods. If the positive thrust of pluralism is to force attention onto intellectual uncertainties, deep disturbance of personal beliefs is likely to result. Perhaps the individual can only cope with the psychic strain involved if he is sustained by some sort of community. Indeed, Nisbet (1971) has argued that a community sustained by dogma (beliefs held to be beyond the need of constant verification) is a necessary condition for the success of the academic enterprise. With today's nine-to-five multi-versity more nearly approaching to *Gesellschaft* than to *Gemeinschaft*, it may be necessary to build into teaching methods formal periods of reflection, of critical permissiveness, of exploration and exposure of basic assumptions, if students are to become aware of the complex and subtle type of commitment implied by pluralism and embodied in university procedures. Pluralism may appear negative—an ideology of perpetual indecision; but its positive thrust is to open all beliefs to examination. Political fanatics know this, and attack the apparent formlessness of universities, often by strategies which hide basic issues behind a smoke screen of apparently 'democratic' procedures.

The essential characteristics of the plural thrust may, as this chapter has shown, be discovered in, and valuable for, forms of higher education other than the university. Indeed, education of all sorts can, and does, take place through many agencies. *Every* institution of society has some kind of educative function, though it may not be recognised as such; conversely, education has a constant tendency to become institutionalised. What are the distinguishing characteristics of an educating institution and what form of authority can it claim in contrast with other institutions of society?

CHAPTER EIGHT

Authority and the Educating Institution

A social institution may be defined as 'a patterned set of social relationships directed towards a definable set of social objectives' (Martin, 1970, p. 35). Every social institution—family, church, factory, office, sports club, etc.—has an educative function because each new generation of individuals must be taught the requirements of their roles in the institution and the expectations which society has about the institution. Through education for roles, the values of a society are made manifest. It is a question of perennial interest (recently revived by Ivan Illich, 1971) to determine which social values in a culture require specialised social institutions—educating institutions—for their dissemination. But, for present purposes, the important point to urge is that social values are only intelligible as the requirements of specific roles and that implicity, if not explicitly, every educating institution—university, polytechnic, college of education, school, etc.—must formulate its goals, or define its product, in terms of specific types of individual.

To function effectively as an administrative entity, an educating institution must, therefore, achieve at least temporary consensus about the type of person it intends to produce. To determine the nature of the curriculum, it must, in fact, accord priorities in the conflicting goals of society. In a plural society, this task is a problem; but it has been the argument of this book that there is a great need for one type of institution—the university—with a persistently recognisable shape which deliberately tries to maintain the tension between these goals. To reconcile the conflict between competing goals—between competing authorities—the educating institution must itself appeal to a form of authority. What is that authority, and how is it manifest?

The problem will appear in administrative terms to the individual, or academic gathering, whose task is to translate ideas into action. Part of the problem concerns conflict in ideals; part concerns conflicting organisational pressures. For clarity, it is best to separate these out.

(a) *The conflict of educational goals*

The conflict of educational ideals which goes to the making of a curriculum has been interpreted, in this book, in terms of the intrinsic conflict between four major types of goals for higher education: manpower-planning goals; consumer goals; personal goals; and academic goals. For example, the question dealt with in chapter 3 of how the content of professional education should be determined exhibited conflict between all four major goals. Highly specialised scientific education (such as Chemistry) could all too easily fail to satisfy any major goal: in particular, if, in the interest of a wider academic perspective, the university teacher blurs the distinctness of a professional role, by, for example, inducing cultural migration, the conflict may be profound.

Consumer, personal, and academic goals may be in conflict in the study of the humanities. Consumer interest in easily-assimilable techniques of study may clash with academic interest in complex procedures of analysis; and academic interest in scholarly technique may in turn clash with the humane, or personal, interests in the content of literature—personal evaluation by authors.

More dramatically, there is the conflict between ideals of 'objective' knowledge and of 'subjectivity'. Personal goals—to answer the question 'How shall we live?'—may be found in conflict with academic goals—to answer the question 'How shall we know?'—and, in all curricula in the university in particular, there is the problem of providing for a disciplined interaction between disinterestedness, commitment, and belief. It has been important to identify these conflicts in different aspects of education because it is the task of the educating institution to define a curriculum while maintaining a necessary tension between these conflicting ideals. The administrative problem is immeasurably increased and intensified by certain organisational features of higher education which impinge upon the curriculum. Five examples will indicate the strains which universities face as educating institutions.

(b) *Pressures on the autonomy of universities*

Firstly, the struggle of different disciplines for comprehensive power, reviewed in chapter 5 as the question of what distinguishes one discipline from another, manifests itself institutionally as the competition of interest groups for funds, buildings, etc. Because the proponents of each discipline regard their intellectual insights as uniquely fruitful, the resulting domestic conflicts can be remarkably bitter, and considerable political astuteness is required for their resolution.

Secondly, educating institutions are subject to forms of external 'authority'. Money is the most powerful sanction in the exercising of any form of external authority, and it is evident at a mere glance that British universities draw the greater part of their funds from the State, through student fees and direct financing. In a paradoxical and peculiarly British fashion, the University Grants Committee has for an astonishingly long time maintained the assumption, rooted in a very different past, that universities are autonomous bodies. In fact, universities are undeniably subject to the authority of the State: the setting up of new universities after the Second World War was alone abundant proof of the State's power to create (and, by implication, to kill) in the field of higher education. Right up to the present day, universities have remained remarkably free from coercive State authority; but they are vulnerable in this respect, and the situation could change. A recent decline in numbers of university applicants accentuates the impression and advances the danger, as many would see it, of the more coercive and overt exercise of State authority—rationalisation it would be called—over higher education.

Thirdly, in a less official way, potential employers of graduates, particularly large industrial concerns, are able to influence policy if not curricula. For example, the decision in a single year of a large science-based industry not to recruit graduates from the science specialism on which the industry is built, can produce a wave of lost confidence which may affect numbers of applicants several years later, which in turn may affect staff recruitment a few years later still, which in turn may affect curricula options available even later. With external pressures such as these, it may be difficult to maintain the balance of autonomous academic studies. There is no easy solution, and some would see danger as well as good sense in the recommendation made in Britain by the Committee of Vice Chancellors and Principals in 1974 that, in view of shortfalls and imbalances in university applications, there should be closer and more methodical consultations between employing bodies and universities.

Fourthly, a constraining authority is also exercised by institutions with no commercial or business interests at all. Bodies such as the Science Research Council, the Social Science Research Council, or the Schools Council can, by initiating schemes, giving or withholding grants, or stipulating conditions, materially affect the work that goes on in a university. For example, Science Research Council bursaries earmarked for students of a one-year taught Masters Degree course, could encourage a university to maintain the course, with consequent effects on recruitment of staff, on balance of teaching interests within a department, and subsequently, therefore, on the shape of the undergraduate curriculum. The erosion of internal authority by such bodies could be the more threatening because it is in intention benign.

Fifthly, universities have to share their authority with professional institutions. The curricular problem of defining the content of professional education has already been noted; there is an organisational correlative. Professional institutions—in, for example, law, medicine, engineering—may specify conditions for entry to a profession, including the passing of examinations. By recognising, or failing to recognise, specific university courses as entitling individuals to exemption from parts of the professional examination, the institutions may affect the curriculum. For example, Council of Engineering Institutions sets an examination called 'The Engineer in Society', to pass in which is a requirement for membership of, for example, the Institution of Mechanical Engineers. The autonomy of universities or other institutions of higher education in determining what the intending professional should learn about the social implications of his studies, may be strongly affected by the existence of such a paper, and the understandable desire of students to gain exemption from it by taking courses of study approved by the CEI.

(c) *Authority in universities*

In coping with these conflicting pressures, it is appropriate for universities to appeal to their own particular type of authority. This is not the place for an elaborate exegesis of the different types of authority, nor for an examination of the detailed power structures which they imply. Adequate treatment of these matters is available elsewhere. For example, philosophical aspects of authority as it appears in educating institutions have been examined by R. S. Peters in *Authority, Responsibility, and Education* (1959) and in *Ethics and Education* (1966). Political aspects of authority (i.e. who runs the universities) have been thoroughly expounded by G. C. Moodie and R. Eustace in *Power and Authority in British Universities* (1974).

A few comments concerning types of authority are, however, necessary before one can identify the institutional implications of the plural thrust, the positive tolerance, which chapter 7 argued is the university's unique contribution to culture.

Authority may be thought of as the right or power of persuasion or constraint in the fields of social order, ethics, knowledge, or skill, which is possessed by a person of special status. Following Max Weber, three major types of authority are commonly identified. *Charismatic* authority stems from exceptional qualities of an individual's personality, often of supposedly supernatural origin; it is associated with 'natural' leaders in times of psychic, physical, economic, ethical, religious, or political distress who do not necessarily possess any form of expert knowledge. *Traditional* authority relies upon piety for what actually, allegedly, or presumably has always existed; commonly it is absolute and 'patriarchs' demand unquestioned deference. Traditional authority is sometimes accepted irrationally if the system of inviolable norms on which it is based is considered sacred. Finally, *legal–rational* authority depends upon a shared belief in the validity of legal statute and functional competence based on rationally created rules. It is the authority of experts who appeal to limited and specific types of information open to public scrutiny and rational questioning. It is with this last, legal–rational authority that university work is, of course, chiefly concerned.

There is, however, a difficulty. It has been argued that a discipline is not suitable for incorporation in the university unless it points to uncertainties. How can one be authoritatively uncertain?

The answer to this question is peculiarly important to the present discussion. Authoritative uncertainty stems from knowledge. One can, of course, be uncertain through sheer ignorance; but such uncertainty would be likely to be unoriginal. New knowledge does not thrive on facts; anyone can unearth a piece of information. Rather, new knowledge thrives on theories which point to new areas of enquiry within an intellectual framework. Sheer information is not enough. It is illuminating to contrast, for example, the sort of knowledge of electronics possessed by a radio ham with that possessed by a university lecturer in electrical engineering, or the knowledge possessed by an antiquarian with that possessed by an historian. University teachers may know fewer facts in absolute terms than other people interested in the same subject areas; but their knowledge (their certainty) is highly structured. And it is the theoretical structures, generating new areas of enquiry, which make their uncertainties (their lack of knowledge) authoritative.

From this observation, several points follow. Firstly, the authority of the teacher depends upon the subject-matter of his studies. Although the intellectual construction he puts upon the subject-matter may be peculiar to his discipline, there is a givenness in the subject-matter which constrains his work. Secondly, universities may be co-adult participatory communities; but it is absurd to expect undergraduates to know as much as the faculty about what is worth studying. Students must, of necessity, trust the faculty to prescribe a syllabus. Thirdly, and relatedly, the authority accorded to university teachers cannot be legal–rational in the strict sense, for students do not have the means of knowing whether a lecturer's treatment of a subject is authoritative. Where complex theories are involved, it is usually not possible to see the force of the theory, its comprehensive power, until much information has been accumulated.

The balance is a delicate one. It does not involve domination of the student by the teacher. The appropriate image is, perhaps, that of an orchestra—with the teacher as conductor and the students as players. Each member of the orchestra will have his own direct response to the subject-matter; but the teacher controls the interaction of his students with it through procedures in which they acquiesce. No doubt some students will quickly see more fruitful ways in which the subject-matter could be approached. Indeed, much of the excitement of university teaching depends upon the ever-present possibility that students will make original contributions to a discipline in the course of their studies. But what must be stressed is that the personal authority of the teacher is accorded to him by colleagues and students on the basis of his knowledge, and his ability to tolerate uncertainty.

The institutional authority of universities depends uniquely on their being seen to cope adequately with uncertainties in a variety of fields. The perception that this is what universities are all about offers a guiding principle with which to tackle the conflicts of ideals and the organisational pressures discussed above. Research and scholarship are instantly seen to be central university activities: the transmission of intellectual certainties, 'facts', to be peripheral. Any idea or activity which threatens to limit the pursuit of theoretically fertile uncertainties is a threat: any offer of funds or personnel which enriches the possibilities of analysis is to be welcomed.

Other institutions in society deal in 'certainties'—and, as I have already argued, have their own educative functions. Churches promote religion: universities teach theology. Political parties manipulate power: universities study political theory. Industry relies on technology: universities carry out research in engineering. The contrasts, although tenuous, are critical. Obviously, there are considerable areas of overlap between the interests of the different types of social institution and those which I argue are central to universities. Indeed, while the university as *institution* is committed to uncertainties, individuals who work there may not—indeed one might say cannot—be. University people cannot help but have strong personal beliefs in religion, politics and so on. Indeed, their beliefs may drive them to their chosen field of study and, in turn, be strengthened by that study. But, the social value which is institutionalised in the university is unbelief—or, more positively, tolerance of contradiction.

This plural thrust, which makes the university a creative centre in modern society, is, however, only one feature of contemporary culture. There are many areas of agreement and, consequently, many aspects of culture which can be communicated by specifically educational institutions where theoretical uncertainties are unnecessary. While it might be argued that exposure to the sort of uncertainties with which university disciplines deal might well be part of all forms of education, it does not follow that different sorts of institution of higher education should be amalgamated. Universities commonly have an amorphous, if not anarchic, structure; too rigid an administrative shape can severely and damagingly inhibit free and flexible development of studies. But other types of educating institution may require a teaching and administrative structure more closely related to the social sub-environments which they serve.

Special types of educating institution might, for example, be suitable for the training respectively of police, nurses, and accountants. For many occupations within these professions, study of what is authoritatively *known* is probably of greater practical value than study of what is authoritatively thought to be *uncertain*. This is not to say that it may not be desirable for the police to study criminology; or nurses to study medicine; or accountants to study economics. If universities are indeed creative centres of culture, their preoccupations should permeate all forms of educational enterprise. But this is quite different from homogeneity of institutional form. The contemporary fashion for vast institutions, far from facilitating free movement from one type of educative encounter to another, may actually inhibit it. The department, or more significantly the research section, has become the natural social unit in some large institutions. The multiversity may suit the accountant's computer; but as 'a patterned set of social relationships directed towards a definable set of social objectives' it becomes less and less comprehensible to the individuals in it. Consequently, they group together in cliques which, although perhaps not officially recognised by the administration, define possible social inter-actions.

I have already urged the value of an engagement–reflection pattern as a way of achieving a fruitful interaction between commitment and detachment; but the pattern is unusual in universities and must be artificially contrived. The value of sandwich schemes in polytechnics and technological universities (formerly colleges of advanced technology) is undisputed; the only limitation on their development is the difficulty of arranging suitable work-placements. What is probably undesirable in most situations where education is for a specific job is to remove individuals from places where the job is done, to specialised institutions remote from day-to-day concerns. It is important to decide what is to be expected of an educating institution. There may be great wisdom in providing for a flow of *individuals* in and out of different types of institution—action-oriented or theory-oriented; conversely, there may be great folly in blurring the functions of viable *institutions* by such muddled concepts as that of the 'comprehensive university'. If the benefits of institutionalised scepticism are wanted, better, perhaps, to take the university to the people, than remove the people physically to the university. This, in fact, is precisely what the Open University has done. First reports (see, for example, Tunstall, 1974, and Ferguson, 1975) indicate that the formula of making it possible for people to attend university while still working at their job is effective academically and highly popular socially.

The institutional authority of universities, then, is seen to reside in a high degree of specialisation of function. It is not just that 'when everybody is somebody, then no one's anybody'; damage is done to the self-esteem of individuals and to the viability of institutions when more is expected of an institution than its social structures are designed to cope with. No doubt these views seem reactionary in the extreme. But enormous amounts of financial waste and personal frustration might be saved if these matters were more widely understood. Many individual and social purposes may indicate the value of a period of university study—but only if these purposes can be temporarily submerged in an intellectual style which emphasises institutionalised scepticism, and a positive tolerance of theoretical perspectives which may contradict the positive thrust of such purposes.

The model of accorded authority which has so far been given may seem perverse. Surely, universities are bureaucracies par excellence! And did not Weber maintain that bureaucracies depend upon legal–rational modes of authority? The distinction between legal–rational authority and the authority which is accorded to university teachers is so slight that there is considerable danger of confusion—a danger which has led, in recent years, to unnecessary and often violent conflicts between students and their universities.

Bureaucratic procedures are undoubtedly appropriate to depersonalise the authority of teachers in matters of university examinations. There is sufficient emphasis on the known even in disciplines of considerable theoretical uncertainty for a legal–rational mode of authority to be appropriate. But that is probably where legal–rational domination should end in the transactions of universities. As will be argued below, selection and assessment are the principal institutional embodiments of the ideas implicit in university education. However, in recent years, bureaucratic control has extended to many other aspects of students' lives.

(d) *The nature of an academic community*

Clark Kerr (1963, p. 20) has characterised the modern university as a series of individual faculty entrepreneurs held together by a common grievance over parking. And it is undoubtedly true that universities nowadays are more readily recognised as bureaucracies than as anything else. Halls of Residence, refectories, parking lots, etc., are all commonly administered by the same corporate structure as administers examinations. Much confusion results from this. 'The university' may be deeply resented when rents for rooms are raised, or when refectory services collapse or become too expensive. But all these matters are irrelevant to the university's chief concern. Indeed, one might almost go so far as to suggest that universities should hand over their accommodation units to independent housing associations or trusts which, no doubt with students on their board of directors, would administer them in the best interests of the community at large —not necessarily just the community of undergraduate students. Similarly, refectories and parking lots could be put in independent hands. In short, all 'housekeeping' arrangements which distract from the university's central task might usefully be abandoned. Following the argument to even more unpopular lengths, one might suggest the ditching of student health-services, social workers, counsellors, and all the clutter of the new maternalism. Certainly, if teaching styles encouraged proper encounters between staff and students they might well be rendered unnecessary.

Of course, retention of all these facilities could, for all I know, be defended on economic grounds; but that would be a different matter. Munificent private donors or a generous local or central government might offer facilities for a university campus—sport centres, arts centres, concert halls—for the cultural enrichment of an area. It is unjust, in social terms, that such luxuries should be provided for the exclusive benefit of university students; but it does make sense to site such facilities where they are likely to be intensively used.

Similarly, it is obviously desirable to provide for the physical and social welfare of large numbers of young people. However, nothing but confusion can result when a bureaucracy which serves the university in its primary task seeks to extend its domination to matters irrelevant to the university's main concern. Students rightly challenge the university's right to dictate their personal styles of life. More importantly, gross distraction from crucial activities may be involved when university personnel muddle with management. Other social institutions can, and do, rightly concern themselves with young people's spiritual and moral well-being and with the administration of plant. The colleges of Oxford and Cambridge were founded, not by the university, but by monarchs and other charitable individuals to minister to the needs of poor scholars. Perhaps this separation of function should be rediscovered.

Yet, does not higher learning require community sustained by dogma (beliefs held to be beyond the need for constant verification) for its pursuit? Certainly. What is at issue is the nature of the community required for higher, and in particular, university education. This is precisely the point. A good community is held together principally by three things: myth, visibility of purpose, and companionship. None of these requires specialised accommodation or homogeneity of life style in every detail. I know few colleagues who feel really relaxed in the superficial mateyness of the student union bar; and I would imagine that few students feel any more at ease sipping the professorial sherry. Nor are myth and visibility of purpose to be found in the shared enthusiasm for the exploits of the university rowing club. Cultural uniformity and community are not the same thing.

Myth is a complex concept. Here, it will be restricted to the justification of a social organisation. It is highly dependent upon the second requirement of community: visibility of purpose. But it is more than that: it comprises elements of the past—knowledge of how purposes previously construed have been carried out, of the achievements of the institution. Purposes are, by definition, concerned with the future; yet aspirations feed on recollections and the celebration of the past may be a potent force in shaping a future. Companionship, the third desideratum, I would suggest, is to be sought in a shared concern with the business of study. That is to say, it is not a deliberately constructed chumminess, but more likely the by-product of something else. I have already suggested (in the previous chapter) that in the *Gesellschaft* university there is a great need for periods of reflection to be deliberately and systematically incorporated in courses of study, so that the types of personal commitment implicit in university strategies of academic detachment can be made manifest and explained. It is from such periods of discussion between teachers and taught that a sense of community must come. Goodness knows there will be plenty for teachers and taught to discuss—particularly if engagement–reflection patterns of study are used. Something similar is often to be found in the shared experience of laboratory or studio or field work. No need for stagey encounters which embarrass everyone.

(e) *The ritual rehearsal of academic values*

But if stageyness is to be avoided, drama is to be welcomed! Ritual is the acted counterpart of myth, and deeply held beliefs are deepened by, as well as expressed by, symbolic interactions. Indeed, the intuitively-perceived authority of universities is manifest in the ceremonies which punctuate their life. Many of these, significantly, centre on assessment.

A student's experience of university begins and ends with assessment. In universities, there is a huge investment of time and funds in interviewing, entrance examinations, yearly examinations, finals, external examiners, etc. Universities are, above all, accrediting institutions, respected for their ability not only to assess knowledge, but also to assess individuals in relation to that knowledge—even though it is knowledge of a specialised sort. To decide what is to be assessed is to decide what finally matters. And a degree ceremony is the colourful culmination of the assessment procedure. It is literally a rite of passage. The student is ritually admitted to a new order of being in the presence of the full community. Hierarchic orders, based on achievement in knowledge, are manifest in styles of dress and positions in procession. Myth is manifest. Purpose is visible. Companionship, if of a rather formal sort, is contrived.

Such ceremonies may seem anachronistic, and indeed they are often ignored by students and mildly tolerated by the faculty. But if, as creative centres of plural culture, universities are to offer a positive tolerance of uncertainty, achievement must be recognised and applauded. Solemn ceremonial may no longer be appropriate. Contemporary forms of symbolic interaction are, however, emerging to take their place. For example, the inaugural lecture of a new professor is a rite of passage of a different sort. Commonly, the lecture provides the occasion for a party and the text of the lecture is often published. Perhaps similar techniques could be applied to the achievements of more junior members of the community. Public presentations of pieces of work, and their subsequent publication in a college periodical, give the appropriate sort of recognition to what the academic community must surely value.

What is required is suitably modern ritual, for ritual puts ideas into action. And a university is an idea—not a place. It is defined by its calendar and its people, not by its buildings. It should theoretically be possible for a university to move and become invisible. Hastings Rashdall (1936, Vol. 1, p. 336) has described how in the Dispersion of 1229 the masters and scholars of the University of Paris, resenting injustices meted to them by the ecclesiastical authorities, simply left Paris for nearly two years. It is ironic that nowadays the occupation of administrative buildings should be believed to be a crippling blow to a university. The fact that pursuit of knowledge in modern times requires vast arrays of equipment and that bureaucratic procedures are required to administer them should not distract one from the centrality of the idea.

By concentrating thus on the institutional embodiment of the idea (the patterned set of social relationship directed towards a definable set of social objectives), one is forced to consider the purposive nature of higher education. Because the purposes of individuals differ, conflict is inevitable in universities and other institutions of higher education. More importantly, universities thrive on uncertainty. If everything were known or knowable, there would be no uncertainty —and no conflict. Consensus, however, implies certainty. That is why consensus may be more dangerous to universities than conflict.

Bibliography

Archambault, R. D. (ed.), *Philosophical Analysis and Education.* Routledge and Kegan Paul, London, 1965.

Ashby, Eric (now Lord), *Technology and the Academics.* Macmillan, London, 1966.

Avorn, J. L., *University in Revolt: a History of the Columbia Crisis.* Macdonald, London, 1968.

Bernstein, B., 'On the classification and framing of educational knowledge'. Chapter 2 of *Knowledge and Control,* ed. M. F. D. Young. Collier-Macmillan, London, 1971.

Bradbury, Malcolm, *The Social Context of Modern English Literature.* Blackwell, Oxford, 1971.

Caplow, T. and McGee, R. J., *The Academic Market-place.* Basic Books, New York, 1958.

Christopherson, Derman, *The University at Work.* SCM Press, London, 1973.

Collier, Gerald, 'Syndicate methods: further evidence and comment', *Universities Quarterly,* 1969, Vol. 23.

Committee on Manpower Resources for Science and Technology, Department of Education and Science, *The flow into employment of scientists, engineers, and technologists.* (The Swann Report) Cmnd. 3760. HMSO, London, 1968.

Council for Scientific Policy, Department of Education and Science, *Enquiry into the flow of candidates in science and technology into higher education.* (The Dainton Report) Cmnd. 3541. HMSO, London, 1968.

Crouch, Colin, *The Student Revolt.* The Bodley Head, London, 1970.

Dainton Report, *see* Council for Scientific Policy.

Department of Education and Science, *Teacher Education and Training.* (The James Report). HMSO, London, 1972.

Dyson, A. O., 'Fieldwork in Theological Education'. Chapter 7 of *Education and Social Action*, ed. J. S. R. Goodlad. George Allen and Unwin, London, 1975.

Elliott, P., *The Sociology of the Professions*. Macmillan, London, 1972.

Ferguson, J., *The Open University from Within*. Hodder and Stoughton, London, 1975.

Friedrichs, R. W., *A Sociology of Sociology* (1970). Free Press, New York, 1972.

Goodlad, J. S. R., *Science for non-scientists: An examination of objectives and constraints in the presentation of science to non-specialists*. Oxford University Press, London, 1973.

Goodlad, J. S. R. (ed.), *Education and Social Action: Community Service and the Curriculum in Higher Education*. George Allen and Unwin, London, 1975.

Gouldner, A. W., *The Coming Crisis of Western Sociology* (1970). Heinemann Educational Books, London, 1971.

Holstein, E. J. and McGrath, E., *Liberal Education and Engineering*. Institute of Higher Education, Teachers College, Columbia University, 1960.

Illich, Ivan D., *Deschooling Society* (1970). Calder and Boyars, London, 1971.

James Report, *see* Department of Education and Science.

Keats, John, *The Letters of John Keats*, ed. M. B. Forman. Oxford University Press, London, 1935.

Kerr, Clark, *The Uses of the University*. Harvard University Press, Cambridge, Massachusetts, 1963.

Leavis, F. R., *Education and the University* (1943). Chatto and Windus, London, 1961.

Lipset, S. M., *Rebellion in the University*. Routledge and Kegan Paul, London, 1972.

McCarthy, M. C., *The Employment of Highly Specialised Graduates*. HMSO, London, 1968.

Martin, D. A. (ed.), *50 Key Words in Sociology*. Lutterworth Press, London, 1970.

Minogue, K. R., *The Concept of a University*. Weidenfeld and Nicolson, London, 1973.

Moberly, Sir Walter, *The Crisis in the University*. SCM Press, London, 1949.

Mohan, R., Shields, J., Wield, D., and Goodlad, J. S. R., 'The demand for non-technical studies at Imperial College', *Liberal Education*, 1970, No. 17.

Moodie, G. C. and Eustace, R., *Power and Authority in British Universities*. George Allen and Unwin, London, 1974.

Niblett, W. R., *Universities between Two Worlds*. Hodder and Stoughton, London, 1974.

Nisbet, R., *The Degradation of the Academic Dogma*. Heinemann Educational Books, London, 1971.

Oakeshott, M., *Rationalism and Politics and Other Essays*. Methuen, London, 1967.

Peters, R. S., *Authority, Responsibility, and Education*. George Allen and Unwin, London, 1959.

Peters, R. S., *Ethics and Education*. George Allen and Unwin, London, 1966.

Polanyi, Michael, *Personal Knowledge: Towards a post-critical philosophy*. Routledge and Kegan Paul, London, 1958.

Popper, K. R., *Objective Knowledge: An evolutionary approach*. Clarendon Press, Oxford, 1972.

Ramo, S., *Cure for Chaos: Fresh solutions to social problems through the systems appoach*. David McKay Co. Inc., New York, 1969.

Rashdall, H., *The Universities of Europe in the Middle Ages*, ed. F. M. Powicke and A. B. Emden. Clarendon Press, Oxford, 1936. Vol. 1.

Reich, C. A., *The Greening of America* (1970). Penguin, Harmondsworth, 1972.

Roszak, Theodore, *The Making of a Counter Culture* (1970). Faber and Faber, London, 1971.

Roszak, Theodore, *Where the Wasteland Ends*. Faber and Faber, London, 1972.

Schein, E. H., *Professional Education*. Carnegie Commission on Higher Education, McGraw-Hill, New York, 1972.

Schools Council, *Sixth Form Survey. Vol. 1. Sixth Form Pupils and Teachers*. Books for Schools, 1970.

Seale, P. and McConville, M., *French Revolution 1968*. Penguin, Harmondsworth, 1968.

Searle, J., *The Campus War*. Penguin, Harmondsworth, 1972.

Shaw, G. B., 'Preface to Saint Joan' (1924) in *The Complete Prefaces of Bernard Shaw*. Paul Hamlyn, London, 1965.

Swann Report, *see* Committee on Manpower Resources for Science and Technology.

Thompson, E. P., *Warwick University Ltd*. Penguin, Harmondsworth, 1970.

Tunstall, J. (ed.), *The Open University Opens*. Routledge and Kegan Paul, London, 1974.

Young, M. F. D. (ed.), *Knowledge and Control*. Collier-Macmillan, London, 1971.

Working Party Members

The names of those who participated in either or both of the two working parties referred to in the Preface (and there was some overlap of membership) appear in the list which follows, together with the titles of the papers which they presented for discussion. Papers marked with asterisks were available to me for the writing of this book. Where substantial sections of my text are paraphrased from papers, specific mention is made in the text; othewise the numbers throughout the text correspond to those against the names in this list and indicate where a particular thought or idea is attributable to a working party member.

The main indebtedness of my text is as follows:

Chapter 3: Peter Tait (35) and Anthony Dyson (8). Few paraphrases are made of Anthony Dyson's paper; but its argument informs the whole chapter.
Chapter 4: Barbara Hardy (14), Denys Harding (13), and Seymour Betsky (3*b*).
Chapter 5: John Coulson (5) and Ninian Smart (31).
Chapter 6: The paper by John Dancy and Kim Taylor (6), although not quoted or paraphrased in the text, emphasised the importance of the Counter Culture for contemporary thought about the curriculum.
Chapter 7: John Coulson (5) and Gerald Collier (4*a*).
Chapter 8: James Robertson's paper (29) was an indispensable focus for thought, although its material was not ultimately incorporated.

(1) Mr R. Andrews
(2) Mr R. A. Becher
(3) Professor S. Betsky (*a*. 'Herzog': a discussion paper.* *b*. The practice of literary criticism: its function in the Humanities *)
(4) Mr K. G. Collier (*a*. Experiments in Moral Education at College level.* *b*. Review of *Professional Education* by E. H. Schein *)

(5) Dr S. J. Coulson (Suggestions on the Theology we ought now to be teaching *)

(6) Mr J. C. Dancy (The Education of the Expert, as seen from the Sixth Form.* Jointly with L. C. 'Kim' Taylor)

(7) Dr W. Davey

(8) The Rev. Dr A. O. Dyson (The future of the expert and the expert of the future *)

(9) Dr D. O. Edge (*a*. Some notes on implicit professionalisation in Science Education. *b*. The engagement of students in the study of value questions)

(10) Dr J. D. Farquhar

(11) Professor J. Ferguson

(12) Mr T. J. Grayson (Some notes on the Soviet Education System *)

(13) Professor D. W. Harding (The Humanities in a University: Standards and Values *)

(14) Professor Barbara Hardy (The Teaching of Literature *)

(15) Professor J. Heywood (Notes for discussion on the American Exemplar *)

(16) Mrs J. Hughes (*a*. A personal note on General Studies in the Sixth Form.* *b*. Some interdisciplinary courses at present available in universities and polytechnics *)

(17) Mr D. Hutchings (The Education of the Expert: an interdisciplinary approach)

(18) Professor F. R. Jevons

(19) Professor L. C. Knights (Literature and the teaching of literature)

(20) Mr K. J. McCormick

(21) Mrs B. Milner

(22) Professor B. Morris (The Humanities and Humanity in Higher Education)

(23) Professor W. R. Niblett (*a*. Higher Education: a dilemma. *b*. Retrospect and Prospect in Higher Education: Some Notes and Queries)

(24) Professor A. Noach (The Arts and the Humanities)

(25) Professor J. A. Passmore (The Humanities and teaching to care)

(26) Professor R. S. Peters (Subjectivity and Standards)

(27) Dr A. T. S. Prickett (*a*. Contextual studies and the integrated day: the paradox of 'discipline'.* *b*. Disconfirming the university *)

(28) Dr Marjorie Reeves (Why History?)

(29) The Rev. Canon J. S. Robertson (The Educating Institution *)

(30) Mr M. J. Scott-Taggart (Ist eine Einheitsuniversität möglich?)

(31) Professor Ninian Smart (The place of Religious Studies in the Humanities and Social Sciences *)

(32) Mr R. Irvine Smith (General Studies for the 16s–18s *)

(33) Professor S. Spender
(34) Mr B. Stableski
(35) Dr P. J. T. Tait (Some reflections on the education of the scientific expert *)
(36) Mr L. C. 'Kim' Taylor
(37) The Rev. Dr G. Tolley (Pressures and interrelationships: professional and statutory bodies and some effects upon education and training of the expert)
(38) Professor H. J. Walton (Current attitudes to medical education, being Chapter 10 of *Contemporary Problems in Higher Education* ed. Butcher and Rudd, 1972 *)
(39) The Rev. G. Whitfield

Index

academicism, 38–40
action, 1, 3, 73, 76, 79, 81
anthropology, 30, 32, 49, 56
Archambault, R. D., 44
Ashby, Eric (Lord), 24, 26
attachment, 65–7, 68
authority, 5, 7, 11, 16, 30, 32, 40,
    48, 60, 65, 81, 84–8
    types of, 10, 43, 84–8
    accorded, 30, 85–8
autonomy, 82–4
Avorn, J. L., 59

Bernstein, B., 49
Betsky, S., 4, 35n, 40–1
Bradbury, M., 55
Brown, J., 3

Caplow, T., 51
chemistry, 15, 16–29, 50, 68
Christopherson, Sir D., 23
Collier, G., 75–8
commitment, 5, 6, 26, 47, 62, 65,
    66, 68, 70–3, 75, 79, 86, 90
community, academic, 88–91
compensatory education, 23–7
conflicts, 5, 16, 31, 47, 48, 69, 82,
    91
consciousness, 2, 25, 60, 63, 65
consensus, 5, 69, 91
Coulson, J., 11, 45n, 73n, 74n
Counter Culture, 59–67, 75

Crouch, C., 59, 72
culture, 9, 10, 11, 25, 26, 28, 40,
    43, 53, 63, 81

Dainton Report, 20
Dancy, J. C., 12n
Davies, C., 11
detachment, 5, 16, 60, 63, 64, 75
Dickson, A., 3
discipline(s), 5, 7, 11, 21, 26, 28,
    30, 40, 44–58, 65, 71, 82, 85
disinterestedness, 36–8, 70–3, 75
Dyson, A. O., 8n, 14n, 26n, 27

educating institution, 5, 56,
    57–8, 81–91
Elliott, P., 17
engagement-reflection, 27–9,
    74–80, 87
engineering, 2, 49, 53–4, 56, 66,
    69, 70, 74, 84, 86
English literature, 2, 5, 8, 15,
    30–43, 55, 56, 66, 68
Eustace, R., 84
experts, education of, 4, 7, 11,
    16–29

fashion, 32–4, 57
Ferguson, J., 87
forms of knowledge, 44, 50, 60
Friedrichs, R. W., 70